Purchased through
a grant from the

BLANDIN FOUNDATION

The NPR Curious Listener's Guide to

World Music

CHRIS NICKSON

Foreword by Youssou N'Dour

A Grand Central Press Book
A Perigee Book

A Perigee Book
Published by The Berkley Publishing Group
A division of Penguin Group (USA) Inc.
375 Hudson Street
New York, New York 10014

Produced by Grand Central Press
Judy Pray, Executive Editor

NATIONAL PUBLIC RADIO
Barbara A. Vierow
Andy Trudeau
Ned Wharton

NPR, npr, and National Public Radio are service marks of National Public Radio, Inc.,
and may not be used without the permission of NPR

Perigee trade paperback edition: December 2004

Visit our website at www.penguin.com

Library of Congress Cataloging-in-Publication Data

Nickson, Chris.
    The NPR curious listener's guide to world music / Chris Nickson; foreward by
Youssou N'Dour.—1st Perigee pbk ed.
        p. cm.
    "A Perigee book."
    Includes bibliographical references, discography, and index.
    Contents: What is world music?—The story of world music—Varieties of world
music—The musicians—The music—World music on CD—The language of
world music.
    ISBN 0-399-53032-0
    1. World music—History and criticism. I. Title: National Public Radio
listener's guide to world music. II. National Public Radio (U.S.) III. Title.

ML3545.N53 2004
780'.9—dc22

                                                                    2004050502

Printed in the United States of America

10 9 8 7 6 5 4 3 2 1

Contents

Acknowledgments

One of the questions I hear all too often when I tell people I write about world music is, "What's that?" World music is immensely accessible and eminently enjoyable. It's been a love of mine for a long time, since I was first intrigued by "Sanctus" from the African folk Mass *Missa Luba* in the late 1960s, when it was used in the film *If.* There's nothing obscure about the music of the world.

I've wanted to write a book like this for several years, to offer an introduction to world music. Now, in doing it, I realize the pitfalls. People are going to wonder, "Why isn't so-and-so included?" (or, equally, "Why is so-and-so in there?"). All I can plead are the constraints imposed by length; it's simply not possible to include *everyone*, and so this has become an overview, a way into world music that I hope will lead people down their own winding, rewarding paths.

I'm tremendously indebted to John Kertzer, who broadcasts

an excellent show on Seattle's KEXP. In a conversation with NPR's Baraba Vierow, he originally recommended me for this project. Thank you.

Thanks also go to editors at various publications for whom I've written about this music: Ian Anderson, Paul Hartman, Mark Moss, Scott Frampton, Bob Mehr, Michaelangelo Matos, John Koenig, Heather Phares, Jeff Tamarkin, Dick Doughty, and Tom May, among others. An extra vote of thanks to Richard Gehr, whose dedication and editing skills when we worked together brought huge improvements to my writing.

I'm grateful to other writers in world music, too numerous to mention, whose work, in both features and reviews, has illuminated and sometimes changed my views.

At NPR, thanks to my producers at *All Things Considered*, Rekha Murthy, Quinn O'Toole, and Bob Boilen, and to Barbara Vierow. At Grand Central Press, Judy Pray has put up with my calls, gladly discussed ideas, and has been a rock.

As always, my agent, Madeleine Morel, has been wonderful.

Friends have made excellent sounding boards for ideas, and their support is always valuable, as is the Leeds United e-mail list, a form of daily therapy and sanity.

Finally, my family: My wife, Linda, has put up with years of "I just want to play this for you" without complaint, and loved a lot of what she's heard. She's also been an excellent critic and proofreader. My son, Graham, has suffered in silence—but I've seen him enjoy the occasional track. My mother has always believed, and I'm very grateful for that. And Brindle, who was always at my side when I wrote, died while I was working on this, but the spirit of the best dog in the world lingers over the book. And now Pepper has become our lovely girl.

This book is dedicated to my late father-in-law, Robert

Avery Hornberg, who died in December 2001. It's hard to imagine a kinder, more generous soul, and this world is a poorer place without him.

Chris Nickson

Foreword

by Youssou N'Dour

W*orld music,* as a phrase, as a category, rings truest for
me when it is celebratory. When we speak of *world
music* as a conceptual gathering of the great musical traditions of the planet, if we do so with a wide-eyed respect for
the richness and diversity of musical forms in our world, our
speech implies an openness, it implies the very sort of inclusive searching by musical souls, which has always nourished
musical discovery in every culture.

Whether in encounters among musical forms from across
the globe or in the preservation of age-old canons of local music making, there is, in the ascendancy of the world music
phenomenon, a common aim, which is to recognize musical
performance from places and peoples outside the beaten path
of Western media hegemony, to elevate styles and traditions
outside of the historically dominant Western categories (be
they classical, jazz, folk, or rock) to a place of more privileged
access to the hearts of audiences throughout the world. As a

performer, it is very exciting for me to be part of an artistic tendency that seems to have taken on, in our times, a life of its own. Whether or not the prediction of Chris Blackwell (founder of Island Records) that world music will become "the classical music of the twenty-first century" holds true, I think it is indisputably true that the repertoire of great music from around the world has already claimed a more significant share of the serious music lover's attention. The very existence of the present volume is a demonstration of this.

As I invite you to delve into the offerings of this inspiring catalog of world music, I cannot restrain myself from wanting to offer a cautionary plea as you begin. If you are to celebrate world music, as this book and I would call you to do, leave behind the trifling definitions and quasi-doctrinal arguments about purism ("roots") and fusion ("sprouts") in the music that abound in world music journalism and critical literature—though not here in this book. These will prove to be an annoyance, a relic of bad colonialism, and ultimately a damper on your enjoyment of the works described in this book. Allow yourselves, instead, the immediate experience of as much of this music as you can *on its own terms*. World music—all of these musics of the world—is living, breathing, evolving, and performance based. In all of these musics, you will find some element of risk and some allure of the unexpected. You will find satisfaction in that which is in them, to borrow Duke Ellington's famous expression, simply "beyond category."

Happy reading and listening!

Senegal's Youssou N'Dour, eldest son of a griotte (praise singer), is a bandleader who, in much the same way as Louis Armstrong did for both jazz and the American popular song (and with similar controversy), has revitalized both popular and traditional music in his country through the inclusion of traditional elements in newfound modern arrangements.

Introduction

People discover world music for any number of reasons. It might be something they hear on the radio, a memory of a foreign vacation, or even curiosity about a particular culture or place. Or they might arrive by a more circuitous route, step by step as they seek music with more depth and meaning than they've found on commercial radio.

But as welcoming as world music can be, it can also be daunting. Over the past fifteen years, the world music section of every record store has grown tremendously, packed with delicacies from around the globe. But with so much of it out there, where can anyone start to make sense of it all? Just because the sound of Congolese rumba gets you smiling and starts your feet twitching doesn't guarantee you're going to want to swing around the room to a Swedish polska.

Separating the wheat from the chaff is purely subjective; it exists only in the ear of the beholder. And as genres increasingly come together, with musicians from all over collaborating and blurring ethnic and geographic lines, it becomes even more so.

The world is a very small place these days. At the beginning of the twentieth century it seemed vast and mysterious, so much of it still relatively unexplored. One hundred years later it's all been mapped and trodden. We can watch wars and conflicts as they happen; the world is, it seems, in the palm of our hand. Still, for however local everything has become, that doesn't mean we *know* it. The music of a country, a region, a people, is a way of discovering more. It takes us beyond the news, beyond the map. It's intimate.

At the start of the 1980s, "world music" was still largely the province of ethnomusicologists. A few areas, like reggae and salsa, were in the popular domain, but most were still ensconced in academia. Now it's an industry, served by magazines, marketing, and record labels that specialize in the genre. World music has its big stars, a very few of whom, like Senegal's Youssou N'Dour or Cuba's Buena Vista Social Club, have even briefly crossed over to commercial success.

Where a single, catch-all world music section was once ample for a record store, now it takes up yards of space, subdivided by continent, country, and artist. There are even categories for those who fall outside any easy pigeonhole. It might be small potatoes compared to the money to be made from Top-20 acts, but world music is one of the few areas of the music business that's continuing to grow. The proliferation of festivals around the country that include or focus on world music keeps awareness and interest high.

More and more people are continually discovering and enjoying world music. Electronica bands have made it a part of their lexicon, sampling ethnic instruments; taking on board borrowed melodies, rhythms, and instruments; and bringing in a young crowd. The Latin music boom, although it was essentially pop music in colorful clothes, introduced another element and left an audience more open to more authentic— but equally exciting—forms of Latin music. These are starting points, and people who are interested will work back to the sources, much as many did with the blues by discovering it through groups like the Rolling Stones, then finding Muddy Waters and John Lee Hooker, before following history all the way to the Mississippi Delta.

Nor is world music something out there, across the ocean. It's at home, too. America is the proverbial melting pot, and immigrants keep home alive with music. The Mexican subculture, in particular, is very active, as stars such as Los Tigres del Norte and Vicente Fernández sell millions of albums and fill arenas, completely under the radar of the mainstream U.S. media. Native American music, Cajun, and zydeco all continue to flourish, and find wider audiences than ever before.

Whatever the reasons, people of all generations are looking outside the menu the media offers to find things *they* want to hear. It could be the plucked notes of a Chinese pipa, Balinese gamelan, or a Tejano polka. Anything we find and enjoy binds us closer to the world, and helps us see the bigger picture. The world might grow smaller by the year, but its joy is still very large.

The NPR Curious Listener's Guide to

World Music

ONE

What Is World Music?

World music is, by its very nature, a sprawling term. After all, it refers to the music made around most of the globe. But when we talk about world music, what do we mean? The most succinct definition, from *fRoots* magazine, is "local music from out there," which certainly encapsulates the ethic.

To narrow it down a little more, world music can take any form, from the most ancient acoustic rites to music with inflections of pop, rock, hip-hop, or electronica. It doesn't need to be traditional music, but it should have an awareness of its roots. Without that anchor, it's simply more modern music aimed at the charts. What's not classed as world music, at least for the purposes of this book, is most American roots music, such as blues, gospel, or country, or their babies, rock 'n' roll. They could arguably be mentioned, but they've spread far enough into the mainstream to deserve their own full books, and inclusion here would cause everything to be compressed.

In addition, those forms have spread across the U.S., while Cajun and zydeco, for example, remain very much based in Louisiana, especially among the French-speaking population, while klezmer and polka offer peeks into small immigrant subcultures. And jazz, of course, is a form unto itself.

Music develops, and traditions become renewed and expanded by successive generations. But it's really only in the past one hundred years that music other than classical has been accepted, collected, and codified. Prior to that the styles were simply folk forms, the voices and sounds of the people, not deemed to be worth a great deal of attention.

But, to quote Louis Armstrong, "All music is folk music. I never heard no horse sing." It's the heartbeat of all popular forms of music. And everything that's happened since has grown from it.

In other words, there's really no easy definition of *world music.* That may well be because it's inclusive, rather than exclusive: Any genre whose breadth reaches from the overtone throat singing of Tibetan Buddhist monks to the programmed beats and loops of the British Asian Massive needs to be elastic in its definition. It's far more than entertainment. It's sociology, a look at the traditions of a country or region, and the way music can express ritual, sacred ceremonies, or politics.

Whether they realize it or not, most people who listen to music have at least a passing acquaintance with world music. There was George Harrison learning the sitar from Ravi Shankar and using the instrument with the Beatles. Bob Marley, still Jamaica's greatest icon, helped make *reggae* a household word, to the point where the off-beat emphasis is instantly recognizable. And in the past two decades, the sound of Celtic fiddles has filtered all across the Western Hemisphere, with the glorious fire of jigs and reels.

That's not to say world music is part of the musical main-stream. It remains very much on the margins in the United States, and that's where it's likely to stay. The occasional album, like 1997's *Buena Vista Social Club*, will strike a chord (in this case, nostalgic, with a good story), and sell millions. But many, many world music artists will sell less than five thousand copies of their latest CD in America.

It's a side of the business of world music that we don't see, or even think about, as we break open a new CD by a favorite African artist and sit back to enjoy it. What does happen, though, as we listen, is that on some level we increase the cultural ties. We broaden our horizons. We become more empathetic. We're thinking outside our own borders and experience and traveling somewhere new, somewhere well outside the box.

World music can also be a political force, bringing the news to your ears in a way no radio report ever can. To hear hip-hop from young Arabs in the Gaza Strip, or the music of an Afghani rubab player who is able to take out his instrument for the first time since the Taliban took power, is to get a fresh insight into the way the world really works. It takes you inside people's lives and makes everything personal. Suddenly you're connected. Connections stand close to the heart of world music. Traditions might have begun in isolation, but other elements help them grow. It could be sounds and instruments traveling along the Silk Road trade route that crossed Asia and the Middle East. It could be the path of the Romany people, or Gypsies, migrating from Rajahstan across the Balkans and Europe, or the Arabs bringing their music to Spain, where it lingers in Andalusia. It could be slave ships, bringing Africans to toil in the New World, or freighters criss-crossing the Atlantic, their sailors carrying the latest records from the Congo or Cuba to play at home. A musician is influenced by everything he or she hears, and the cumulative effect changes music on a regional level. Music can be a beacon for a tribal, national, or regional identity (such as happened in Mali or Guinea after independence in the 1960s), and a celebration of who people are.

That carries over into the languages involved. Music develops locally or regionally and is named in the local language — and that's the way it goes into the world. Even an instrument such as the thumb piano can have several different names (mbira, ilimba, kalimba), depending on where in Africa you are. It can be confusing, perhaps, but it remains respectful of people and their traditions.

In a time when so many things seem prefabricated, from the slight variations on the sound-alike and dance-alike teens that rule the charts to the lowest common denominator global economy of fast food and beverages, world music offers an alternative. There's no cookie-cutter sound or style. The lively juju of Nigeria's King Sunny Ade definitely isn't the sultry bossa nova of João Gilberto. But both work.

Just by the law of averages, not everyone is going to like everything in world music. Some sounds are definitely harsher on Western ears than others; the pentatonic scale so widely used in West Africa, which is the basis of blues and rock, seems perfectly natural and normal; but to most, Chinese opera can be a cacophony of grating noises. And that's fine. No one's expected to enjoy everything. As long as your ears and your mind remain open, you'll find plenty to spark your imagination and leave you smiling.

We talk about the music of different countries and tend to associate a certain style with a nation, such as flamenco with Spain or cumbia with Colombia. But it should be remembered that while a nation might have a predominant musical style, inevitably there'll be a lot more happening within its borders. Nor is any particular style likely to end at passport control; borders are, at best, arbitrary political creations, having little to do with the reality of humanity. If anything, music has more of a tendency to be regional—and a region can be anything from a few villages to part of a continent—a quick investigation of Balkan music can offer a prime example. With variations, depending on the particular makeup of the population, certain recognizable styles cross five or six countries.

Some who delve into world music just stick to one area, gradually going deeper and deeper in their explorations. For some it could be a connection to their ethnic origins, for others simply the way the music catches their ear. There's so much musical wealth to be tapped out there that it's easy to devote years to specific styles or regions.

Others are generalists, taking a little from here, a little from there, and building up a mosaic of global music. By a manner of association, one thing can lead you to another, going from the sound of the Arabic oud to flamenco guitar to Argentinean tango.

Quite simply, there's no right or wrong way to listen to world music. Approach it as you want. Start with the big names or just from some curious item that you came across somewhere. Whatever your point of entry, the new vistas start opening immediately.

Like any musical genre, every year world music has its big albums. It could be a new record by a major star, an old band getting back together (as has happened in recent years), or the stunning debut of a new act with a long career ahead. World music continues to expand and grow. A lot of older music is being reissued on CD, digitally remastered with excellent sound.

Other organizations, such as Global Sound, are taking archives and slowly making them available online. It's already possible to have access to a staggering amount on world music. Because this genre doesn't generate the huge profits (or expenses) of pop, it has been able to remain a relatively pure area. People aren't in it to get rich but for the love of the music they make, because they're committed to it.

And, in a world that seems to worship youth, age is no barrier in world music. *Buena Vista Social Club* made international stars of a set of people old enough to draw pension checks. Many artists don't hit their creative peaks until their forties, fifties, or even older—well past the time that conventional pop music would view them as acceptable "commodities." But at age ninety, Cuba's Compay Segundo had more to offer than many singers seventy years his junior.

For anyone who wants more than he or she is being fed by much of the mass media, world music can be a refuge. There's substance, beauty, and often a great deal of spirituality to be found.

Ultimately, the enjoyment of it is a purely subjective matter. It's what hits you, what moves you. The world is out there, waiting.

TWO

The Story of World Music

T he term *world music* became part of the common currency in the mid-1980s. By then, with the popularity of Paul Simon's revelatory *Graceland* and the somewhat rootsier *The Indestructible Beat of Soweto* introducing the world to the wonderful sounds of South Africa, it was apparent that something was happening that stood outside the main current of pop.

That was, perhaps, the starting point for much of the modern interest in world music, but, simply, world music has been around as long as people have been inhabiting the globe.

At first there was voice and rhythm—handclaps or feet stamped on the ground to accompany a dance. Different tribes and peoples developed their own chants, then songs, and unique rhythms to accompany them.

As the nomadic populations moved, their music moved with them, which could account for similarities in the music of the Sami (or Lapp) people of the Nordic countries and the First Nations of North America, who arrived over the Bering Land Bridge before the continents parted.

Instruments—struck, plucked, bowed, and blown—tended to come with settlement and time, as civilizations developed. But it's been the movement of people, voluntary and otherwise, all through history, that's changed the course of music. When West Africans were brought to North Africa as slaves, they eventually altered the shape of music there. And as the Islamic Empire spread across North Africa, the Middle East, and into Spain, their music followed as well.

The trade route known as the Silk Road, which ran from the Middle East across Asia and into China, transported more than spices and goods. Music traveled in both directions, with influences taken onboard and gradually absorbed.

The story most people know is of African slaves coming to the Americas, and how their music gave birth to blues and jazz. That's true, but it's only part of the tale. What's often forgotten is the slave population throughout the Caribbean, Central America, Peru, and Brazil (which had more slaves than the United States). They also influenced the music that grew around them. Without slavery we wouldn't have reggae, samba, blues, or the rich variety of Cuban music. But four hundred years of human misery is a very high price to pay for even the most beautiful sound.

Every wave of immigration—whether it's within a country, throughout a continent, or across an ocean—changes music. It might be slight, and it's certainly gradual, each one a grain of sand, but eventually those grains of sand build up, and you have a new beach.

Where World Music Began

Perhaps the greatest tale of travel and musical influence is from the Romany people, better known as Gypsies, although they consider that term derogatory. Their origins are in the Indian province of Rajahstan. When Muslims tried to invade India in the eleventh century, some of the Romany people moved West—whether fleeing or as part of a military force routing the foe is uncertain. However, they did stay on the move, through the southern Caucasus and into what is now Turkey. Eventually, probably as part of a force from the Ottoman Empire, they entered Europe through Armenia, spreading through the Balkans, into Greece, then gradually farther west, with their first appearance in Europe being around 1300 C.E.

Wherever they went, their music went with them. Its root was in India, but as the people traveled, they took in new ideas and, in turn, influenced local musicians. Thanks in large part to the Romany people, for example, the world has Spain's flamenco music, whose very deep roots trail all the way back to India. But this influence was just as great throughout the Balkans and central Europe. Oftentimes, it was the Romanies who were the musicians playing at weddings, village feasts, and celebrations of saints' days. They learned the local repertoire and added their own touches, which in turn became part of the local lexicon. The musicians would travel throughout the region, earning a living from their instruments, playing with other musicians, and absorbing and influencing sounds. Indeed, during the nineteenth century it wasn't uncommon to see Romany and Jewish musicians playing klezmer music side by side in central European villages—or even playing it alone, if Jewish musicians weren't available. Klezmer took on some of the characteristics of Romany music, and vice versa.

The term *world music* was first used in 1889 at the Paris Exposition Universelle, where music from Indonesia (then Java), Japan, and Vietnam could be heard. For the citizens of Paris, celebrating the centenary of the French Revolution, it was indeed a brave new world. For most it confirmed their Western superiority. But some, like the composer Claude Debussy, were taken by the possibilities of these new sounds.

Over the next twenty years there was a realization by people that their heritages were slipping away as the world changed, and rural traditions slowly died with growing urbanization and mechanization. In England Cecil Sharp and others began collecting folk songs, and people across Europe did much the same. In Hungary it was the composer Béla Bartók. He'd made his first folk song transcription in 1904 and gradually let its influence infuse his music; from 1912 to 1914 he did little but travel around Hungary, collecting folk songs.

The First Recordings

The true revolution in music, on a global scale, came early in the twentieth century. The start of professional recording meant that songs and performances could be preserved in more than written or oral form (and very few folk musicians read music; traditions have generally tended to be oral and imitated). And record companies weren't slow to see the possibilities of recording in many parts of the world.

It wasn't altruism, the chance to document and preserve traditions for future generations, that motivated them, although that has proved to be the long-term corollary effect. Instead it was nothing more than commercial opportunity. The thinking was that people would pay to own recordings of their local music. And so the big record companies of the day

The World on Your Turntable

Ethnographic music albums had been available since the LP form began. Moses Asch's Folkways label issued plenty, and in the mid-1950s Columbia released the eighteen discs of the *Columbia World Library of Folk and Primitive Music,* collected by musicologist Alan Lomax. In 1954, independent Elektra Records brought out *Voices of Haiti.* But the idea of an America record company focusing on the music of the world didn't take off until 1967, when the Elektra spin-off label Nonesuch began its Explorer series. Under the guiding hand of the late Teresa Sterne, who ran Nonesuch, Explorer eventually ran to a total of ninety-two albums, taking in everything from the mbira (thumb piano) of Zimbabwe's Shona people to Japanese solo shakuhachi flute. Invitingly packaged, with extensive but easily readable sleeve notes, the series formed an entryway into foreign music for a generation of Americans, taking it, for the first time, out of academia and into the living room. It was music to be listened to and enjoyed, rather than dissected. Pioneering in its vision, the Explorer series created the precedent in America for much of what would become world music.

opened offices in Egypt, India, and many other countries. Technicians and equipment were dispatched across the globe.

The equipment of the time was bulky and unreliable, and the finished recordings extremely fragile. Some of the journeys the technicians undertook were long and grueling—one 1909 expedition spent several months crossing the Caucasus and penetrating deep into the heart of Asia, working its way along the old Silk Road. But the results were a revelation. Recording time might have been severely limited, as musicians used to playing for hours found themselves restricted to a couple of minutes, but there was no denying the power of the music or its popularity. Very few people in non-Western countries might have been able to afford early gramophones, but it seemed as if they all purchased the local recordings. A few copies were available in Western countries, but there was little demand for this ethnic music there.

That's changed with time. These days, many of these recordings, often in states of disrepair, are being tweaked and remastered in state of the art sound labs, with the best of them being issued on CD. Instead of mass consumption—the curious pop music of the day—the major audience now tends to consist of ethnomusicologists. However, many of the discs make fascinating listening, a brief glimpse through a window into a world that's both familiar and long vanished.

These ventures did kick-start local recording industries, however, which grew over the decades from the late 1920s onward as phonographs became more widespread. These local recording industries were the key to the real development of regional music, in addition to the idea of performers as personalities. By the 1940s, radio was the main way of disseminating music. Popular artists sold more records and gained more recognition as a result of radio play. Their careers soared and in some cases could reach tremendous heights. For Um Kulthum, still Egypt's most popular diva more than a quarter century after her death, it meant recordings, a string of films, and Thursday night radio concerts that would virtually bring the Middle East to a standstill, as everyone crowded around radios to listen.

Recordings also had an importance besides popularity. Those early musicians whose playing was disseminated and heard influenced all the players who listened to them. So several generations of Irish fiddlers, for example, have bits of Michael Coleman's style in their playing. And because recordings were permanent, the version of a tune on disc tended to become definitive, rather than changing as it was passed along.

That altered the entire folk process. But it was only one of many changes that were occurring, transforming music and the world. Economic opportunity, pogroms, world wars and their aftermath caused mass migrations. In the late nineteenth and early twentieth centuries, the United States filled with a polyglot of European immigrants, who brought their traditions and music with them. In particular, Jewish klezmer music flourished in America far more than it ever had at home. In 1948, when the *Windrush* docked in England, bringing the first real West Indian immigrants, it set in motion the wheels that have given us British calypso, reggae, and jungle.

The Influence of Trade

Trade has had a profound influence on music. After World War II, ships plied the Atlantic route between Africa and the Americas, and sailors would carry the latest records from one country to another, selling to musicians and fans in the ports. The bands would bring those latest tunes and styles into their own music, adapting them to their own music. Cuban music, in particular, proved to be popular in West Africa, a real source of inspiration. In the Congo it sparked Congolese rumba, which would eventually speed up and become soukous. The Senegalese tended to play their Cuban music a little straighter, and it stayed popular until the 1970s, when homegrown sounds began to replace it. Even now, Senegal's recently re-formed Orchestra Baobab plays with a strong Cuban lilt.

The traffic wasn't just in one direction, though. Across

West Africa, bands were recording, and those discs made their way to Cuba, where they altered ideas of percussion and rhythm, deepening and thickening the Afro-Cuban sound.

The First Rise of Latin Music

Latin music, and Cuba in particular, was something of a focal point in the 1950s. Back then, Cuba was a playground of casinos and entertainment, not the enemy it became after the revolution. Its music stood for fun, good times, and dancing. The polyrhythms were irresistible. The first explosion of Latin music hit the United States in the late 1940s with the mambo, popularized by so many artists, from Machito to New York–born Puerto Rican timbale player Tito Puente, who kept stoking the Latin boom through the popularity of the cha-cha-cha in the 1950s. Rather than listening music, it was dance music, as couples filled halls around the country, and the beat of the congas blared out of radiograms. It was a fad that lasted until the mid-1950s, dying down as rock 'n' roll turned into pop music and decided that it really was here to stay. But fads and fashions had long driven popular music, whether it was swing, the jitterbug, or any of a dozen others that had come and gone. The next one would have a more lingering effect, perhaps because it passed into jazz rather than remaining in the pop mainstream.

Bossa nova had hit Brazil in 1957, when composer Tom Jobim and singer/guitarist João Gilberto joined forces. The music they produced was a revolution that built on samba, softening it with jazz, blurring the edges and round the corners. Ostensibly simple and lightweight, the perfect background music, it was actually complex, both rhythmically and melodically, with many of the pieces containing poetic lyrics. It reached the United States largely through two songs,

Astrud Gilberto's "The Girl from Ipanema," which evoked the warm beaches and sensuality of Río, and "Desafinado," covered by jazz saxophonist Stan Getz. The music arrived in the early 1960s, an era when people were striving for the upwardly mobile executive lifestyle with its patina of sophistication, and the big social gathering was the cocktail party.

With its lulling rhythms, soft sound, and rich melodies, bossa nova was the perfect soundtrack for those events. That was especially true after the jazz musicians who followed in Getz's footsteps, sensing the possibilities of the music, took it up. For a while it seemed almost *de rigeur* for a jazzman to release an album of songs with a bossa beat.

While that offered one path, it also took bossa into the cul de sac of easy listening music and ended up condemning it to a musical wallpaper role in America. It would be many years before the United States went back and reexamined the roots of bossa and discovered how deep they ran.

African Independence

Meanwhile, in Africa, countries were beginning to take on their own identities. Throughout the late 1950s and early 1960s came independence from the colonial powers, and with it the desire for national expression. It wasn't uncommon for the new governments to fund "orchestras" to play and explore the music of the country—it happened in Mali, Guinea, and in several other places. In many ways, it was a necessary step toward shaking off the shackles of the past. And while a mix of bureaucracy and music can often be horrible (as in Russia or China), in most instances it worked. In Mali, for example, there was the history of the Sundiata epics to be examined, as well as many regional traditions. These were all actively encouraged, and the result was some glorious music that was truly African, owing little or nothing to the white masters who'd ruled for so long.

The Power of the 1960s and 1970s

In the West, no one was really looking toward the music of the world at large. Little exotic pieces of it came into brief contact with America, but that was the extent of it. The world was changing, though, thanks in large part to the Beatles, who put up the signposts for a generation ready to ask questions and look outside themselves.

To most people in the West, India was little more than another country on the map before the Fab Four. But by the middle of 1967 almost everyone was familiar with the name of their guru, Maharishi Mahesh Yogi, and George Harrison's sitar teacher, Ravi Shankar. Indeed, the knock-on effect of Beatle fame was such that Shankar had become a star in his own right, playing at pop festivals and headlining tours across Europe and America, playing Indian classical music.

Only a small number of Beatles fans made the jump to Shankar, but it was enough. And the whole world heard George plucking the sitar on "Norwegian Wood" and "The Inner Light." Suddenly rock musicians were hunting for sitars (and people to teach them how to play it) and other exotic instruments. And they were looking outside their homeland, listening and realizing that the world had far more to offer than they'd imagined before. The feeling even extended outside rock, with some of the more adventurous jazz musicians, like John Coltrane, making their own ventures into Indian music.

Rolling Stone Brian Jones hit the hippie trail to North Africa, specifically Morocco, where he'd record the Master Musicians of Jajouka, a group whose unearthly sounds and rhythms had been the music of Morocco's court a few centuries earlier. And when an album of their music appeared, albeit heavily tweaked in the studio by Jones before his 1968 death, the patronage of a famous rock star meant they were on the map, taken seriously and remembered.

Compared to the generations of musicians who'd come before, rock performers showed a rare and eager curiosity about the world. Cream drummer Ginger Baker went on to study African drumming. Traffic and Blind Faith singer/keyboardist Steve Winwood made an album with Nigerian high-life musicians in the early 1970s, long before such fusions became fashionable. And they were merely the tip of a large iceberg.

But it wasn't only people in Britain and America who were looking beyond their own borders. The mid-1960s brought political and social turmoil to Brazil as a military government established a dictatorship in a left-leaning country. Young musicians and artists were pushing at the boundaries as the Zeitgeist of the time spread. Singer/songwriters Caetano Veloso and Gilberto Gil spearheaded the iconoclastic movement known as tropicália. Along with some like-minded colleagues, they tried to internationalize Brazil's inward-looking popular music (known as MPB), bringing in electric guitars, and elements from rock. However, their efforts met with critical and governmental resistance, to the point that the pair was exiled for four years, finally returning in the 1970s. Ironically, Veloso is now one of Brazil's leading figures, and Gil was named as the country's minister of culture.

The social changes of the 1960s had created an atmosphere that was more open to ideas, which probably helped the breakthrough of Bob Marley in 1973. He, along with singing partners Peter Tosh and Bunny Wailer, made up the Wailers. They'd been stars in their native Jamaica for a decade, coming to prominence during the era of ska music, keeping the hits coming as the music developed through rocksteady and into reggae. At the end of the 1960s, they worked with producer Lee Perry to develop their sound. What they created found full flower on *Catch a Fire*, the first reggae album to be marketed like rock.

Reggae, of course, was the music of Jamaica, but it also had an audience in Britain, not only among the West Indian population, but also many Britons. Some reggae songs made the charts and had since 1964, when Millie's "My Boy Lollipop" had been a ska hit, not only in the United Kingdom but also in America.

Catch a Fire upped the ante. It was a definite gamble, but it ended up paying off in a style that couldn't have been imagined. It started the rapid arc of Marley's global stardom. To many around the world, he *was* reggae, its voice and face— and, in his writing, its militant heart. He made reggae part of the standard musical vocabulary of the United States, and in Africa he was an icon, a symbol of the African diaspora. His African tour in 1980, a year before his death, was a major event, going to a continent most big stars had been happy to ignore. It was his inspiration that started African musicians on the reggae trail, to the point that two of them, Lucky Dube and Alpha Blondy, have become international roots reggae stars in their own right. The legacy of Marley still casts a long shadow, not so much in reggae itself, which has morphed into the dancehall style, but in the spirit of the music; for many, many people everywhere, his remains the name that springs to mind whenever the genre is mentioned.

The 1980s and World Music

It was in the 1980s, however, that world music really began to gather momentum. At the start of the decade, former Genesis

When Reggae Crossed Over

Chris Blackwell, the head of Island Records, knew instinctively that Bob Marley and the Wailers' take on reggae had the ability to reach a wider audience. His goal was to make it popular with the white audience already tuned in to progressive rock. Blackwell had financed *Catch a Fire*, which the band recorded in Kingston, Jamaica. A longtime supporter of Jamaican music (he'd grown up on the island and had once been saved from drowning by a group of Rastafarians), he loved the mixes he heard. But he also knew they wouldn't work for the market he envisioned; they were still a bit too raw, in need of a touch of rock polish. So he took the master tapes back to Island's studio in England, where he brought in keyboard player John "Rabbit" Bundrick and American guitarist Wayne Perkins to help smooth out the sound and give it "more of a drifting, hypnotic-type feel than a reggae rhythm." In addition to the six-string, Perkins added pedal steel guitar to "Stir It Up," and Bundrick's clavinet rounded out "No More Trouble." Remixed, with the bass toned down a little, it became the landmark recording that broke reggae into music's mainstream. The original Jamaican album remained unreleased until 2001, when it was issued in a two-CD pack with the final version.

vocalist Peter Gabriel, now enjoying a successful solo career, helped found WOMAD (World of Music, Arts and Dance), an organization geared toward staging festivals that would offer artists from all over the opportunity to play. Music from other parts of the world would be just one ingredient in the whole. The first of these, held in 1982, wasn't a success; indeed, it took a concert reunion of Genesis to bail Gabriel out of his financial hole. But he'd been willing to put his money where his mouth was and gamble all.

That same year, two intriguing records hit the market. The first was a collaboration between David Byrne, the singer for New Wave band Talking Heads, and British avant-garde pop figure Brian Eno. *My Life in the Bush of Ghosts* (which took its title from a novel by Nigerian author Amos Tutuola) brought together funk with samples drawn from radio broadcasts around the world. It was groundbreaking, the first exercise of its kind, and helped open some ears to the idea that other cultures existed, with plenty of valid things to say. It set some listeners on a path of discovery.

The second disc was far less oblique. Nigeria's King Sunny Ade had long been the star in his homeland, the main figure of the style called juju. Among his innovations was the introduction of the pedal steel guitar—an unlikely instrument, but it worked, and gave his percussive music a distinctive sound. After the death of Bob Marley, Island Records was casting around for someone to follow in his footsteps, someone to capture both white and black audiences. King Sunny received the nomination.

Juju Music appeared in a flurry of publicity. It was a critical success, a sound new to the West but still very accessible. However, it didn't capture the attention of the people who really mattered—the record buyers. Ade built a cult audience, but couldn't move beyond that. But it helped place Ade, and African music, on the map.

For many African musicians, Paris was the place to be in the early 1980s. The French had discovered African music and its natural ability to get people dancing. But they wanted the beat faster and the production slicker, more in line with European standards. A number of West African singers and musicians moved to Paris, singing and playing on the glut of records that emerged during the decade. While all too often the product was formulaic and soulless, sometimes everything clicked. And it made the African musical presence quite visible.

Every small movement forward was a gain, however, and another one came the following year with the seminal release *The Indestructible Beat of Soweto* (the album was issued in the United States in 1986). South Africa's Apartheid policy had brought about isolation and a cultural boycott. This album, the roots music of the black townships, which had previously gone unheard in the West, sounded a clarion call. There had been South African stars before, people like Miriam Makeba and Hugh Masekela, but this was a new generation, full of fire and anger.

The record received plenty of radio play in Britain and throughout Europe. In the United States its impact wasn't anywhere near as large, but a few people definitely noticed something was happening.

Going to Graceland

One who noticed was Paul Simon. As half of Simon and Garfunkel, then as a solo act, he'd been a major star for much of the 1960s and 1970s. More recently it seemed that his muse had deserted him, and he needed fresh inspiration. The music of the South African townships seemed to offer that.

Breaking the cultural boycott and recording part of his album in South Africa was no small step. But Simon did it to make *Graceland*, the record that resurrected his career and proved to be the boost for South African acts like Ladysmith Black Mambazo to jump to the international level. Regardless of anyone's opinion about his political actions, there's no doubt that Simon's multiplatinum disc meant that millions of people heard the music of South Africa. And in concert, to his credit, he often let the spotlight fall on the African artists.

More than any record that had come before, *Graceland* opened the door for an awareness and acceptance of world music, even if it wasn't going by that name—yet. That would effectively change in 1987. A London meeting of several people involved in this as-yet-unnamed business coined the phrase, rejecting alternatives like *worldbeat*. It was never meant to be anything more than general (and certainly, even today, there are plenty of people who hate the term), but it offered a category under which to put—and market—all this global music that couldn't be easily categorized.

The timing was certainly good, as interest in world music was beginning to rise. World music sections started to appear in larger stores. It even had its first real star, a Senegalese singer named Youssou N'Dour. He'd appeared on *Graceland* and added backing vocals to Peter Gabriel's big hit disc *So*. Following that, he'd toured as Gabriel's opening act, before co-headlining the Amnesty International Human Rights Now! tour in 1988—the only African performer among a plethora of Western artists. That led to his acclaimed major label debut, *The Lion*, in 1989, showing his trademark, rhythmic mbalax style. But among real aficionados, his reputation had been made earlier in the decade with the stunning *Immigrés*, on which his high, part-griot wail exploded over the beat and the chattering sabars in stunning fashion.

Gabriel had not only helped N'Dour's career, he'd also proved to be a vital mover and shaker for the whole industry. He'd demonstrated his interest in and commitment to world music with WOMAD, and non-rock musical elements had crept into his albums. His high profile as a star meant that the things he did brought attention, so when he began Real World, which was a studio, record label, and multimedia company (with the WOMAD headquarters on the same campus in the village of Box, England), the albums his label released were newsworthy. He broke artists like Pakistani qawwali singer Nusrat Fateh Ali Khan, Anglo-Indian vocalist Sheila Chandra, and many others through to a bigger audience, taking them to the next level. And when his own, adventurous *Passion* appeared in 1989, it exposed even more of his fans to the world music he'd used as his inspiration. As the soundtrack to director Martin Scorsese's controversial film *The Last Temptation of Christ*, it used samples, rhythms, and ideas from around the globe. Gabriel then took it one step farther by issuing *Passion: Sources*, which aired the original tracks he'd used as his launching pad for *Passion*.

Both sold well, helped in part by the controversy the film, which greatly outraged the Catholic Church, generated. And they raised the growing awareness of the wealth of music that was out there to be discovered.

Peter Gabriel wasn't the only rock star with strong inclinations toward world music. Since the demise of Talking Heads, David Byrne had been exploring other music and finding much that resonated with him in Brazil. In 1989 he founded the Luaka Bop label, beginning with the compilation *Brazil Classics 1: Beleza Tropical*, a solid introduction to the Brazilian musical climate of the prior three decades. He expanded from that foundation, covering more of Brazil and the Afro-Peruvian tradition, including the remarkable diva Susana Baca.

The 1990s

As the decade changed, the stage was set for world music. It had some big-name advocates and, in the baby boomer generation, an audience that still loved music but was feeling alienated from modern rock and hip-hop. World music offered them substance, melody, and more than a touch of the exotic in their lives.

Given those factors, it was perhaps ironic that the first big breakthrough of world music in the decade should have come from banging, hyperactive Jamaican dancehall music. Shaggy's remake of "O Carolina," which had been an island hit for the Folkes Brothers in 1959, cruised into the American charts in the early 1990s. It formed the start of a growing crossover between hip-hop and dancehall that helped make American stars out of artists like Beenie Man, Shabba Ranks, and Capleton. The appeal was to a generation decidedly younger than the boomers, but the effect was the same.

The 1990s was also the decade that saw the return of Latin music in America. Since the boom of the 1950s, it had played a very minor role, peeking in for a while with Santana's early work and in the rootsier Mexican material of Los Lobos. What came to the fore this time around, however, wasn't the mambo or the cha-cha-cha but pop music with a Latin sheen, as Gloria Estefan scored hit after unstoppable hit. But although the chart successes of the boom were strictly pop, be they Luis Vega or Shakira, the Latin boom did at least allow other things to sneak in.

It especially helped Mexican regional music become more visible, bringing corridos and mariachi a little way out of the barrio, and allowed the danceable axé of Brazil's Daniela Mercury to thrive. But with an ever-increasing Spanish-speaking population in the United States, it was only fair that this should receive an airing—and eventually the clamor became loud enough for the Latin Grammy Awards to be created.

The decade's biggest world music story was also Latin, although it was distinctly lacking in glitz. Instead, it was perfect testament to the idea that music isn't solely the province of the young, as a group of Cuban musicians and singers, the vast majority of them past retirement age, gathered and made 1997's *Buena Vista Social Club*. It was blatantly nostalgic, harking back to the lush music of the 1950s, richly melodic and gentle. The singing and playing was of the highest caliber, even though many of the participants hadn't been inside a studio in years (in the case of the late Ruben Gonzalez, many years had passed since he'd even played a piano, but that didn't stop him performing with stunning brilliance). The accompanying documentary by acclaimed director Wim Wenders helped push the record over the top, with some seven million copies sold worldwide. It also made international stars of the artists as they toured throughout Europe and the United States.

In the wake of *Buena Vista* came the flood of Cuban recordings. Not only did many of the album's participants release solo records but suddenly anything Cuban became marketable. While some good music made its way out, the sheer glut of product essentially undervalued everything.

World Electronica

At the other end of the musical spectrum, in the world of electronica, world music had also been warmly embraced. After the initial, beat-driven thrill of raves had worn off, musicians needed more variety and substance in the work they were creating. Sampling rhythms and sounds from other cultures was one way and led to the subgenre of "ethno-techno," championed by bands like Britain's Transglobal Underground.

It was inevitable that, if they continued, these bands would be led deeper into world music; and indeed many were, exploring the music of different regions within their own sounds. And within different world musics, electronic scenes rose. The Asian Underground (now known as the Asian Massive) started

in London. Within a couple of years it had become a galvaniz-
ing force for young British Asians, as it gave them their own
musical identity, which had morphed into the hippest sound
around, lauded on both sides of the Atlantic.

Perhaps the most commercially successful world electronica
band to date has been Afro Celt Sound System, who have
mixed Celtic-inflected melodies with African rhythms, backed
by loops, samples, and techno beats. As early as 1991, Scots
band Mouth Music had made the first forays into the same
sound before veering off into other directions, and the Afro
Celts built on that to define and develop their sound. The boom
in dance music and electronica gave rise to other scenes, like
the Arabesque of the North African Diaspora, and different
rhythms and beats filling the dance floor in different parts of
the world. But hip-hop really became music's universal language as the world headed toward the millennium. From its
origins in America (with a strong influence from Jamaica), it
spread across the world. And, initially, it was U.S. hip-hop that
had the wide appeal, but it wasn't long before rappers and DJs
from all over were coming up with their own rhymes and beats.
Often they'd incorporate native instruments, making their
sound local and unique. Styles developed globally, from France
to India, South America to Africa, where the music seemed
almost like a homecoming. In South Africa it entwined with
house music, creating a popular hybrid called kwaito. Throughout West Africa the regional overtones became strong, and the
violence and misogyny so prevalent in American rap was replaced with more positive thoughts and words.

In the New Millennium

Events in the new millennium changed many things in the
world, but the United States has been especially hard hit,

with a growing feeling of isolationism that developed in the wake of 9/11.

World music in America has slowly been struggling to recover from that day. Albums still have been released, but some of the general momentum has been lost in the country's mood of isolation from much of the world.

It hit hardest with touring foreign artists. With the tightened security regulations, obtaining visas has become much harder, sometimes impossible. Even renowned artists who'd toured many times, like Cuban pianist Chuco Valdés, were unable to get permission to enter the country. It took longer, often months, to secure a visa, if it were even possible.

The appetite for world music remains, however. The music itself continues to expand as people work in their traditions, reinterpreting them or creating hybrids that mix styles in ways no one could have imagined just a few short years ago. And there's also the thriving business of reissuing seminal albums, such as the Nonesuch Explorer series, which first introduced many people to the music of different continents.

In an age of increased globalization, in which countries and economies sometimes seem joined by the idea of profit and lowest common denominators of culture, world music offers something deeper. Unlike so much chart fodder, it remains the sound of the heart and spirit.

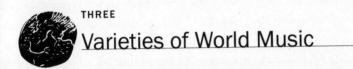

THREE

Varieties of World Music

The varieties of world music can seem almost limitless. And the only way to approach it all seems to be by continent or major geographical region. Even then, influences, ideas, and styles tend to be regional and ethnic, rather than national. That flow can be seen more easily by working through a continent rather than by laying everything out alphabetically. Africa begins with West Africa, the cradle of so much music and home to the styles most familiar to Westerners.

Africa

To some aficionados, African music *is* world music. It's an understandable reaction. The roots of so much that's familiar—from blues to jazz to rock—lie in the syncopated rhythms and pentatonic scales of West Africa that arrived in America with slavery.

But African music, as such, doesn't exist. The rough, raw raï of Algeria is completely different to the lush Zulu choirs of South Africa, and Kenya's famous dry benga sound bears little resemblance to the Mande music of Mali.

Like every continent, it's filled with myriad different sounds as local traditions have grown and developed. In some places, like the massive Big Red island of Madagascar, whose population migrated from the Pacific, the influences of many places have come together to create something unique.

Rich histories abound everywhere, and their weight is often still felt in the music being made today. The cultures are old, and families are justifiably proud of their ancestry and stories.

Postcolonial Africa has faced—and continues to face—political and social problems. The AIDS epidemic is perhaps the biggest challenge of all. It's decimated populations, and some of Africa's greatest musicians, like Franco and Fela Kuti, have fallen victim to it. Dictatorships and rebellions spring up like wild fires to change the course of a country's future. For many people, poverty is endemic, a way of life that's endured for generations and shows no sign of ceasing.

The great powers that carved up Africa might be gone, but the mark they made still remains. Depending on where you travel, English or French can act as a *lingua franca*.

In the 1960s, during the heady first days of independence, several countries tried to find their own identities through music. The governments helped create and fund "orchestras," which were intended to make music that owed nothing to the colonial past. It was both ambitious and inspired, a policy that gave a foundation on which to build a musical future, and some of the great music, especially of West Africa, has been the long-term result.

Few Western stars tour Africa, even nowadays, and going

back a few decades, appearances were even more rare. So it's perhaps no surprise that those who did make the trip exerted a great influence on African musicians. Duke Ellington's concert in Addis Ababa, for example, had a profound effect on Ethiopian jazz, and James Brown's 1974 shows around the continent brought American funk into the music of many young artists—indeed, he brought it home. And Bob Marley's 1980 tour helped consolidate his status as an icon across the continent, and brought reggae alive as a musical style for a generation.

As is true everywhere, individuals have stood out and towered over the music of their countries. Inevitably it's been by innovation, whether the renewal and refinement of traditions, as was the case with a singer like Egypt's Um Kulthum, or adding entirely new, foreign elements, such as happened with Nigeria's Fela Kuti and Afrobeat.

Afrobeat, with its mix of Nigerian high life rhythms and American funk, was perhaps the first cross-cultural fusion, the precursor for much that's happened since, like Taj Mahal's widely praised *Kulanjan*, which connected the dots between Malian music and American blues, showing that the line was very direct and obvious (indeed, the banjo, once the most popular instrument in the United States, originated in West Africa).

All divisions are arbitrary, and there's not necessarily more cohesion among the music of North Africa and the Middle East than there is between other areas of Africa. Nor is the division as simple as religion—Islam remains a predominant faith down into West Africa. It's perhaps more a matter of perception; these are seen as the Arab countries, and can be more easily grouped together.

If there's a music that works across most of the region, it's the style called sha'bi (also spelled as chaabi), a raw street pop that developed from an urban folk form. It's spawned its own offshoot, the popular jeel (or "youth music"), much more pop oriented, with its own stars and heart throbs, like Egyptian Amr Diab.

North Africa's most familiar music, though, is raï, personified by the Algerian-born singer (and longtime French resident) Khaled. More than any other, it's the modern style that's been accepted in the West, often referred to as the "desert blues."

But these two are just the tip of the iceberg. One of the great glories of Arab culture is its classical music, made up of a complex series of maqāms, or scales. It remains very much alive, and Egyptian singer Um Kulthum (whose name has many Western variants, including Oum Kolsoum) is generally hailed as the greatest of the twentieth century, whose voice captivated not only the intelligentsia but the entire population of the region.

Many North Africans—especially Algerians—have emigrated across the Mediterranean to work and live, to the extent that North African ghettoes exist in many European cities, such as the Barbès area of Paris. And the music they've made there, powerfully redolent of their native lands, but with inevitable flavors of their new home, keeps pushing the development of different styles; as the world grows smaller, cross-fertilization can become more important.

Mali, Guinea: Mali gets most of the attention, but Guinea falls into the same catchment area, as the two countries largely made up the Mande Empire, celebrated in the Sunjata (or Sundiata) epic. Made up of three linguistic groups, the old Mande songs, sung by djelis (the musician caste known elsewhere in West Africa by the more familiar griot) remain the core of the region's musical history. Djelis (djelimusos is the

African Reggae

There's no single music that covers the entire African continent; the closest thing would be the Jamaican import reggae, thanks in large part to Bob Marley. His songs spoke directly to the poor and downtrodden around the world, and nowhere more than in Africa. The deep roots of reggae lie in Africa, and Marley's 1980 tour of Africa cemented his status there as an icon.

It also helped fuel the reggae boom. It wasn't unusual to hear African bands slip an occasional reggae-inflected track onto their albums through the late 1970s and early 1980s; and almost every band, however lowly, seemed to have a few reggae covers in their repertoire. It was a music that crossed borders and continued to speak vociferously to everyone.

So it's no surprise that a few artists have dedicated their musical lives to it, particularly to the type of roots reggae that typified Marley's output. Some of them have achieved international fame with the style. Alpha Blondy, from the Ivory Coast (but educated in the United States), has developed a reggae style that leans heavily on the African side, and remains staunchly political in his tirades against oppression and calls for African unity. South African Lucky Dube switched from mbaqanga to reggae in the mid-1980s, using the form to protest Apartheid. Since then his sound has received global acceptance. As hip-hop takes root as the international music of choice among a younger generation, though, it remains debatable as to whether reggae in Africa will eventually wither away.

feminine form) are professional musicians, the keepers of the oral histories, the singers of praise songs, and, traditionally, advisers to their patrons—the people who paid them. It's a hereditary group whose power, really, is knowledge and memory and which was especially vital in the days when little was written down. The most famous djelis have always been showered with gifts from admirers; it's rumored that the reason the great djelismuso Kandia Kouyaté has released only two CDs is that she simply doesn't need the money, as well-wishers have given her not only plenty of that but also houses and even an airplane. It might just be gossip, but it illustrates the great power a select few singers have and the esteem in which they're held.

The majority of djelis and djelimusos work within an established traditional framework of songs, with improvisations that are based on specific formulas. Many tend to use a band consisting of the kora, a harp-like instrument usually with twenty-one strings, whose rippling, lyrical sound has become almost a trademark of Mande music. The n'goni, which in some ways resembles a banjo, is distantly related to the lute, and the balafon is, at heart, a wooden xylophone, although guitar has become a popular addition over the past forty years.

The kora's popularity isn't limited to Mande music; although widely played in Mali and Guinea, it's also widely found in Senegal and Gambia. It can offer melodic counterpoint to a singer or can stand alone. *Cordes Anciennes*, from 1970, was one of the first kora recordings to appear in the West, bringing together three majestic players in a summit performance; almost thirty years later, Toumani Diabaté and his cousin Ballaké Sissoko (whose fathers performed together on the original) joined forces for a follow-up, *New Ancient Strings*. Diabaté has been the most visible and versatile of kora players, releasing solo albums that have taken the instrument into new areas. He led the Malian group that worked with American bluesman Taj Mahal on *Kulanjan*, the widely praised disc that explored the roots of the blues in Mande music.

Completely different again is the music from the Wassoulou region in the south of Mali. Famous for its female singers like Oumou Sangaré, Sali Sidibé, and Nahawa Doumbia, Wassoulou music might sound as if it came from a deep well of tradition, but in fact it's very recent, dating only from the 1950s, and is a combination of local styles, none of which owes anything to Mande music. The singers—and the vast majority of Wassoulou singers are women—vocalize about social problems, love, and the rights of women. The distinctive instrument of the style is the kamelen'goni, or young man's harp, a sort of six-string cross between a kora and a n'goni, which was invented only in the 1950s. Over the past decade it's gained a number of Western fans, principally through the artistry of Sangaré, a songbird who's been forthright in her stance for woman and against the common practice of polygamy.

But perhaps the most interesting stories from Mali and Guinea revolve around the state-sponsored orchestras that came after independence. Before that, the major influence on the dance bands was Cuban music, imported on record, then learned and played by musicians. And that influence remained, to a greater or lesser extent, even in the new bands that sprang up, and whose brief was to explore the Mande tradition.

In Mali, the new doctrine eventually led to the formation of the Rail Band du Buffet Hôtel de la Gare, better known as the Rail Band or the Super Rail Band, which played in the restaurant of the railroad station in Bamako, the capital city. Among its founding members were guitarist Djelimady Tounkara, who still leads the band in addition to maintaining a solo career, and singer Salif Keita, who went on to join Les Ambassadeurs du Motel (also known as just Les Ambassadeurs) before becoming a major solo star.

Since the start of the 1990s the Rail Band has probably spent as much time on the road overseas as it has at home. Guitarist Tounkara, considered one of the best in the world, was lauded in the book *In Griot Time* by journalist Banning Eyre.

Guinea's Bembeya Jazz had come together in 1961, even earlier than the Rail Band. They also played the classic Mande repertoire, with Sekou Diabaté the equal of the Rail Band's Tounkara on guitar. But things began to unravel in the 1970s, when singer Aboucar Demba Camara died in a car wreck, and by the mid-1980s the group had broken up in everything but name. However, 2002 saw a reunion, a glorious new disc, and plaudits as the artists toured, with an announced intention of staying together.

But it wasn't the sound of the new orchestras that ignited Radio Mali after independence in the early 1960s. That honor belonged to singer/songwriter Boubacar Traoré. Born in the western city of Kayes, he'd wake the country every morning, performing his hit "Mali Twist" on the radio. Affectionately known as Kar Kar, for his soccer dribbling skills, he became one of the country's first stars. However, even as he pursued music, he made a living as a tailor, farmer, insurance agent, and many other things. Finally he quit music (many in Mali simply assumed he'd died), and it wasn't until his rediscovery in the late 1980s that he began performing again. Since that time, his career has become international, with a number of albums and frequent tours around the world. Rooted in the pentatonic scale, his music has a bluesy feel that owes little to the Mande tradition.

But neither does the sound of one of the biggest artists to have come out of Mali. Guitarist and singer Ali Farka Touré makes his home in the isolated village of Niafunké, up in the north of the country, on the edge of the Sahara Desert. Yet his spare, monochordal sound has echoed loudly across the Atlantic, where Americans can hear the root of the blues in it—not a million miles from the music of the late John Lee Hooker (whom Touré claims as an influence, bringing the blues full circle). In his work you can hear echoes of the nomadic Tuareg people who inhabit the region, and listening to *The Radio Tisdas Sessions* by Tuareg group Tinariwen only confirms the connection. Touré's *Radio Mali* album, of radio sessions from the 1970s, shows the bones of his style, with his voice and guitar disarmingly simple, yet astonishingly complex, over the rhythm of a calabash. But it was really on albums like *The River*, *The Source*, and his award-winning collaboration with American roots musician Ry Cooder, *Talking Timbuktu*, that his music became known. Largely retired from music since his 1999 release, *Niafunké*, he's used his earnings to help his village and has acted as a catalyst for the career one of of his protégés, Afel Bocoum.

All music needs to be freshened by new blood, and there are impressive young artists who've broken through, both in Mali and on the international stage. Habib Koité has proved to be an impressive singer/songwriter and an extremely talented guitarist (he taught the instrument in Bamako). While modern in his lyrical ideas (his "Cigarette Abana," an antismoking song, was a hit throughout West Africa), his music brings together traditional instruments from different Malian cultures to make something new. So, too, does the rising star Rokia Traoré. A protégé of the unrelated Ali Farka Touré, she's a singer/songwriter whose material synthesizes Malian styles rather than coming from any established tradition; and her smooth, lyrical voice seems to owe more to jazz and European singers (the daughter of a diplomat, she largely grew up outside Mali) than anyone from her homeland. In 1997 she won the Radio France International African Discovery Award, which rapidly kick-started a career that's gone from strength to strength.

Issa Bagayogo takes a different approach. A kamelen'goni player and singer, he mixes his Wassoulou sound with beats, loops, and samples, which are created in a Bamako studio by former Ali Farka Touré guitarist Foumad Koné and French engineer Yves Wernert. The three albums they've collaborated on so far have all sold well at home (earning Bagayogo the nickname "Techno Issa"), while the dance element has helped find a growing international audience for something that's an entry into the future for Malian music.

Senegal: Surprisingly, modern Senegalese music doesn't have very deep roots. In essence, they reach back only to the early 1960s, when the Star Band was the top name in Dakar, with a repertoire of mostly Cuban music and the lyrics learned by rote. They eventually began to introduce some local elements, including songs in Wolof and the sabar (otherwise known as the tama, or talking drum).

The big musical name in Senegal, and the one most widely recognized in the West, is Youssou N'Dour, a man whose career began with the Star Band. It's certainly true that he's a towering talent. But he's far from being the only extraordinary musician from the area. Over the past few decades, Senegambia has proved to be as musically fertile as anywhere in West Africa, producing not only N'Dour but Baaba Maal, Cheikh Lô, Ifang Bondi, Orchestra Baobab, Wasis Diop, Positive Black Soul, and Ismael Lô—a list that just scratches the surface.

Senegambia shares the djeli tradition, and some instruments, with other parts of the old Mande Empire. Here, though, they're known as griots (griottes for women), and their modern-day influence is arguably somewhat less. A former

French colony, the main language of Senegal is Wolof, although French is still widely spoken, and Islam is the predominant religion.

Following the local success of the Star Band, other groups sprang up in their wake, most notably Orchestra Baobab, named for the nightclub where they played. While many bands let their music develop in a more Africanized fashion, Baobab stuck close to the Cuban style throughout the 1970s and into the 1980s; the legendary 1982 release *Pirates Choice* was a high point. After eventually breaking up, they were persuaded to reform, older but still full of melody, in 2001, and even issued a new album in 2002.

The real turning point for Senegalese music occurred in 1977, when the younger members of the Star Band, including an eighteen-year-old singer named Youssou N'Dour, broke away to begin something fresh, energetic, and defiantly Senegalese. The new Étoile de Dakar was, perhaps, the local equivalent of the punk revolution going on in Britain at the time, cutting through everything their elders had done with attitude and griot wails. After just two years they split in two, half following N'Dour's fellow vocalist El Hadj Faye into the short-lived Étoile 2000, and the others backing N'Dour in Super Étoile de Dakar.

This was the band that turned everything upside down. They pushed the talking drums, sabars, forward, letting them chatter across the rhythms, and turning up the guitars. The result was something unique, exciting, eminently danceable—and completely Senegalese—called mbalax. Built on cross-ryhthms traditionally used in talking-drum ensembles, it took dialogues between drums and voices and gave the parts to guitars and keyboard too, making for a full, driving sound.

They weren't the only ones creating something new in the capital, however. Super Diamono, fronted by Ismael Lô (whose preference for playing acoustic guitar with a harmonica on a neck rack often brought an African Bob Dylan to mind), were mixing funk and jazz with mbalax.

Of course, there's more to Senegal than Dakar. Casamance, the southern region—which is almost a separate country, since it's divided from the rest of Senegal by The Gambia—has produced its own stars, notably the group Touré Kunda, although their success has come overseas rather than at home. With a complex mix of styles, some Senegalese, some decidedly not, Touré Kunda became a firm favorite in Paris at the beginning of the 1980s, although their popularity has never extended to English-speaking countries, where they remain a footnote rather than stars.

Like most countries, though, the focus does tend to remain on the capital. But Dakar, with its many clubs, tends to be the incubator for new music, especially since N'Dour, with his Xippi studio and own club, has become a patron of new talent, including dreadlocked singer Cheikh Lô, whose acoustic-based sound owes a lot to older Cuban music.

While Lô is the point man among a younger generation of singers, what's blasting out of the stereos of Dakar's youth these days is hip-hop. It's a scene that's exploded, inspired by American hip-hop. But it's taken on its own coloration, lyrically and musically. The raps are in Wolof or French, and the negative attitudes so prevalent in the U.S. genre have been replaced by positivity—urging youth to keep the streets clean and show respect, for example. Local flavor peeks through in some of the instrumentation—alongside the beats and loops are the sabars, kora, and mbalax rhythms. So far the only act to break out at all has been Positive Black Soul, who has released one album in the West and who contributes a couple of tracks to *Africa Raps*, a seminal West African hip-hop compilation whose focus is largely Senegalese.

It would be remiss to discuss Senegal without a mention of Wasis Diop. A longtime Paris resident, he's displayed a pan-African sensibility on his records (including an excellent Africanized remake of the Talking Heads song "Once in a Lifetime"), working with a number of artists, such as the French-based Tunisian Amina on "Le Dernier Qui a Parlé," her daring 1991 Eurovision Song Contest winner.

The biggest stars to appear from the former British colony of The Gambia were the Super Eagles. Like so many other West African groups, they started out playing Latin music, only turning to their roots in the 1970s, eventually changing their name to Ifang Bondi before moving to Holland after the music scene at home collapsed in the 1980s, following an attempted coup in the country. Ifang Bondi, now with only one original member, still records and tours.

The country has brought forth some remarkable kora players, however. Dembo Konteh and Kausa Kouyate have released a pair of splendid and seminal albums in the west, whereas several others, like Dembo's father, Alhaji Bai Konteh, have been crucial in the development of music for the kora.

Effectively, though, music (even, to an extent, the traditional griot style) has gone underground in The Gambia in recent years, never having revived from a government suppression of clubs in the early 1980s during a political crisis.

Cape Verde: The nearest African port to the Cape Verde islands is Dakar, and that's still a thousand miles away, making the islands an isolated outpost in the mid-Atlantic, where the musical influences of Europe, Brazil, and Africa converge on the former Portuguese colony in the morna style. With a history that dates back over a century, the poetic minor-key songs are fully of melancholy, a sadness (*sodade*, or *saudade* in Portuguese) that seems endemic to the islanders, with its echo of the similar Portuguese style known as fado. While not the only style to emerge from the islands, it's easily the best known. The great popularizer of morna has been Cesaria Evora, whose whisky-tinted voice caresses the music with a fragile elegance and strong heart. The "barefoot diva," as she's known has become a major world music star over the past decade.

Ghana: Once called the Gold Coast, Ghana is best known for the dance music called highlife, which emerged in the 1920s as separate urban and rural styles—the urban being the more sophisticated. Widely recorded, it became emblematic of African music in the 1930s and 1940s and particularly popular with Africans who'd emigrated to the United Kingdom.

Highlife really coalesced and found its voice in the hands of E. T. Mensah, who led the Tempos from the early 1950s on, through their golden years of the 1960s. His big-band approach drew in influences from jazz, Latin, and West Indian music; the group toured all over West Africa to great acclaim. By the 1970s, however, maintaining a big band was no longer economically feasible, and guitar-led highlife bands became the new standard.

While Ghanaian highlife has made little lasting Western impact, one band from the country did achieve renown for a while. Osibisa, the London-based aggregation of musicians from Ghana and the Caribbean, melded rock with African rhythms with great success at the beginning of the 1970s. Indeed, for several years, they were a beacon for many African bands, a sign that international acclaim was indeed possible.

But by the start of the 1980s they'd largely become a spent force after trying to please the changing tastes of their record companies.

In fact, most of the big names in Ghanaian music have been expatriates. Master drummer Obo Addy, based in the United States, and percussionist Mustapha Tettey Addy, who divides his time between home and Germany, have kept the country's rhythms very visibly vibrant on the international stage.

Ghana's other big musical contribution is the relaxed genre known as palm wine music. An ancestor of highlife, it's remained a laid-back, acoustic genre, although its popularity has steeply declined over the years. One of the best-known palm wine musicians was Kwaa Mensah, although nowadays Koo Nimo is perhaps the greatest living exponent. Like many other styles, it's crossed borders, and the late S. E. Rogie of Sierra Leone scored a hit across Africa in the 1950s with "My Lovely Elizabeth" before moving to the United States and then to the United Kingdom.

Benin: Benin is home to a couple of obscure musical traditions, neither of which has found much support within the country. Instead, Benin is more readily known as the birthplace of one of world music's best-known female singers Angelique Kidjo. However, after her first international release, 1990's *Parakou,* she began moving away from her African roots and toward the Western musical mainstream, bring jazz and R&B heavily into the mix.

Nigeria: Ghanaian highlife music found a welcoming home in Nigeria for several years and was an influence on Fela Kuti, one Nigerian to find success overseas—although at home he was in constant conflict with the government.

The bigger local style, though, has been juju, which tends to be sung in Yoruba, rather than pidgin English of Kuti's Afrobeat.

Juju music developed into a real urban style in Lagos, the country's capital, in the late 1940s and 1950s. But its launch into the truly modern age came from I. K. Dairo, who introduced electric guitar and accordion into the lineup. Leading his band, the Blue Spots, he created a string of hit singles and was awarded the British M.B.E. for his contribution to music.

In every music, styles change and artists go out fashion. Juju music is no different. By the 1970s, Dairo had been eclipsed by two younger upstarts, Ebenezer Obey and King Sunny Ade, both of whom brought their own innovations— chief among which seemed increasing the number of musicians in their bands to more than twenty.

Obey broke internationally before Ade, but it was Ade who reaped the fame. In 1982, he was championed by Britain's Island Records as the person to be the new Bob Marley. Marley, a global icon, had died the year before, and the label didn't want to try to replace him with another reggae star but to offer something utterly different.

Ade fit the bill. His juju sound had an exciting polyrhythmic flow, the conversations between melody and rhythm were often intoxicating. The pedal steel guitar he'd brought into his band made for a distinctive and unusual sound. When *Juju Music* appeared in 1982, it received excellent reviews and immediately established his name.

However, while that and its follow-up, *Synchro System*, both sold respectably, they didn't launch Ade into the superstar stratosphere, as Island had hoped. To be fair, it was probably wishful thinking that an artist who didn't generally sing in English could attract a massive Western audience.

Instead, he reached the comfortable plateau that he's

maintained over the years, periodically releasing albums and enjoying an upsurge in popularity in the late 1990s as something of an elder statesman of African music. At home his albums are instant best-sellers, and he's the head of the Musicians' Union, in addition to owning his own label and running a nightclub—a veritable business empire, as befits someone who's treated with the utmost respect.

Obey's career hasn't enjoyed such a stellar arc, but he too continues to play and record, putting out excellent discs that rarely receive the exposure they deserve.

Although heavily overshadowed and often deemed outdated, highlife music has continued in Nigeria, following a course that has distanced it from its Ghanaian roots. One of the best contemporary players is a veteran, Chief Stephen Osadebe, whose work is a good as anything to have emerged from Ghana.

Nigeria was also the home of one of the first African musicians to make any impact in the United States. In 1960, *Drums of Passion* by the late Michael Babatunde Olatunji (known simply as Olatunji) created a mild sensation. Quite probably the first African album recorded in America, master drummer Olatunji took traditional Yoruba chants and rhythms and brought them to the New World. At the time it was exotic, a novelty; in retrospect, it was truly seminal, and for many Americans, it represented their first exposure to real African music. Olatunji went on to record with many people, including Grateful Dead drummer Mickey Hart, himself a pioneer in exploring world rhythms. He died in April 2003.

However, no Nigerian artist has had the influence of Fela Kuti. His Afrobeat sound offered a modernized take on African music, bringing in American soul, funk, and jazz on top of highlife. Building on interlocking instrumental patterns, it was

eminently danceable and funky, topped by Kuti's political dia-
tribes, often in pidgin English, which was the Nigerian creole
language. Since his death, his son Femi has put his own twist
on the sound, updating it a little, while being only marginally
less confrontational in his politics.

Cameroon: The country of Cameroon is known musically for
two completely unrelated things—pygmies and being the
home of world music's first star. The pygmies, who still inhabit the forests, are a rural people. *Pygmy* is, in fact, a generic
term, referring to stature, and it actually covers many different groups spread across central Africa. The Cameroonian
Pygmies first appeared on Western radar thanks to Deep Forest, a French duo who successfully mixed lush electronic music with samples of pygmy music. But Deep Forest isn't the
only band to have mixed the music of the Pygmies with other
sounds; Britain's Baka Beyond have created a fusion with
Scots music that works surprisingly well, a seamlessly integrated mix of studio and field recordings that do justice to
both cultures.

The all-female group, Zap Mama, also has deep roots in
Pygmy culture, as leader Marie Daulne spent time there as a
child before moving to Belgium. The influence was apparent
in some of the unusual vocalizing on the band's a cappella debut, *Adventures in Afropea 1*. Since that time, though, they've
undergone personnel changes and broadened their horizons
to take in many more styles, ranging as far as R&B and hip-
hop on more recent releases.

Along the way Sally Nyolo quit the group and embarked on
a solo career. Over the course of four albums, she's developed her own style that remains very strongly rooted in the
music of her home. While she's achieved critical success, no
Cameroonian has had the same musical impact as Manu

Dibango, who became a world music star in the 1970s. With his shining bald head, the singer and multi-instrumentalist has become a pan-African soul, one of the great elder statesmen of world music, whose contributions remain vital. Grounded in jazz, he cut "Soul Makossa" (named for the Cameroonian makossa style) in 1973, and watched it blow up into a huge international hit. Ironically, perhaps, he's better known abroad than he is at home, frequently guesting on all manner of African albums, his voice and saxophone style unmistakable.

The other main Cameroonian style is bikutsi, and as played by Les Têtes Brulées—which translates literally as Burned Heads—it is wild and rampantly energetic. With costumes and face paint, their effect was equally strong visually and musically. However, after just two albums, they disappeared.

Congo: The Congo, under its many various names, has proved to be as important a force in African music as Mali. As early as the late 1940s, musicians in the capital, Kinshasa (the city was the capital of the Belgian Congo; Brazzaville, the capital of French Congo, lay just across the river), were adapting Cuban rumba and adding twists of their own. It wasn't long before small record labels, often owned by European immigrants, began recording and selling the music, one early success being Antoine Wend Kolosoy, whose "Marie-Louise" was one of the first big hits in the style.

Congolese music hit its stride in the 1950s under the leadership of Joseph Kabasele. His band proved to be a crucible for many future stars, including singer Tabu Ley Rochereau and guitar wizard Franco, who served their apprenticeships with him. Using three guitars became an integral part of Congolese rumba. There was a lead guitar, a rhythm guitar, and another to fill the gap between the two, giving a rippling fullness to the music.

In 1956 Franco headed off to form the seminal OK Jazz (whose early hit was the self-praising "On Entre OK, On Sort KO"). He was among the first to exploit the possibilities of the sebene, the break in the song made for dancing. By extending it, often *greatly* extending it, he made it into the focal point of the song, where his flowing guitar picking could mesmerize. As OK Jazz developed, it became the gold standard for Congolese bands. Other excellent guitarists, like Papa Noel and Doctor Nico, emerged in Franco's wake.

Rochereau, too, moved on, forming African Fiesta, which experimented wildly with the Congolese form, and then founding Afrisa, the other major band to emerge from the country.

A faster, harder sound, termed *soukous,* emerged in the 1970s. Rumba was still the base of it all, but the new generation of musicians wanted something more energetic, not as relaxed in its groove. It truly took hold in Paris during the 1980s, after so many young Congolese musicians emigrated there. The technically advanced studios and production put a gloss on the music, and the infectious beat made it a club staple, bringing artists like Papa Wemba and Kanda Bongo Man to stardom. Even the old-timers adapted their sound, and Franco and Rochereau maintained their popularity.

Soukous achieved the kind of popularity rumba had never been able to manage, and it was the first African music to find a real international fan base (in part because much of it was recorded in Europe and released on European labels, which offered better global distribution). Its impact, especially during the first half of the 1980s, shouldn't be underestimated.

However, following Franco's death in 1989, the edge seemed to vanish from Congolese music, and the political struggles and upheavals of recent years have done nothing to help the country's stability. For now, at least, it appears that the golden years of Congolese music have come and gone. But while they were here, they were glorious indeed.

Angola: The fact that Angola's musical traditions are fairly minimal might well be a comment on the country's political problems with civil war, an almost constant factor since independence in 1974. The violence had a huge effect on the music, at times quieting it, but it's never silenced it altogether, and a few artists have remained active.

One who's been very vocal is Bonga. A former professional soccer player, now resident in Paris, he's released several albums that illustrate his Angolan heritage. While there are plenty of similarities to the music of Brazil in his soft sound, the feel remains ineffably African, which is true of another Angolan who's made a small mark on the international scene, Waldemar Bastos. Like Bonga, he lives in exile—in his case Portugal—and has toured extensively. Again, the slightly tweaked Brazilian sound makes his music fresh in the ear.

South Africa: South Africa stands apart from every other country on the continent by having vital traditions not only in rooted music but also in jazz. While South Africa seemed to fall out of nowhere into the Western public eye in the 1980s, the country's influence long predated that—Solomon Linda's 1939 song, "Mbube," became famous in the United States when the Weavers recorded it as "Wimoweh" in 1948, and the Tokens as "The Lion Sleeps Tonight" in 1961. And long before *Graceland*, South African artists like Miriam Makeba and Hugh Masekela had been on the U.S. charts. Both were really jazz artists, but managed to nimbly cross over to pop. In "pure" jazz, pianist Dollar Brand (now known as Abdullah Ibrahim) remains a potent force, and names like Dudu

Pukwana and Chris McGregor helped fertilize the English jazz scene of the 1960s and 1970s.

Until recently, the shadow of Apartheid was a blight on the country, making it hard for African artists to gain widespread acceptance inside South Africa. However, a thriving subculture had developed in the black townships. In the 1930s and 1940s, there was a love of American vocal groups, like the Inkspots and Mills Brothers, which complemented the harmony traditions of the main Xhosa, Zulu, and Sotho tribes (the traditional playing of these and other tribes was documented by musicologist Hugh Tracey on his Music of Africa series of LPs). Groups like the Manhattan Brothers adapted the American sounds and style, often singing in their native language and giving the harmonies a uniquely South African tone. One of the most successful black groups of their time, throughout the 1940s and 1950s they toured around the country and recorded a succession of singles for the Gallo label, all of which were huge hits within their community. For a while Makeba was a Manhattan Sister (then part of the female equivalent, the Skylarks, who had their own hits), and trumpeter Masekela was a part of their band.

During the 1950s, the township style called pennywhistle jive became the new vogue. Performed on the cheap and readily available pennywhistles, it became the predominant music, eventually to be replaced by sax jive, which soon took on the name mbaqanga. Throughout the 1960s the sound developed, especially the distinctive, elastic bass playing, while the vocal style developed out of the harmony sounds of the earlier bands.

Mbaqanga become the sound of the township, and different strands developed, whether it was the "groaning" style of Mahlathini and the Mahotella Queens, where the male bass voice traded lines with female harmonies, or the more electric Soul Brothers, with a great rhythm section and two-part harmonies.

Until the 1990s, mbaqanga typified the sound of black South Africa, finding its widest audience on Paul Simon's *Graceland*. But that album also featured the ineffable and beautiful Zulu harmony of Ladysmith Black Mambazo, showing another, older tendril of the tradition.

Although there was a great divide between black and white in the country, many whites were firmly anti-Apartheid. One unafraid to take a musical stand was Johnny Clegg, who studied Zulu music and incorporated it into his sound, first with Juluka, then Savuka, scoring a global hit in the 1980s with "Scatterlings of Africa."

For many years, though, music of the townships didn't receive much international attention. That changed in 1983, with the compilation *The Indestructible Beat of Soweto*, still one of the most important albums of world music. It brought mbaqanga and other township styles to the world. While not as widely heard as *Graceland*, this is undiluted music, powerful and soulful.

In the new, equal South Africa, the main urban style is kwaito, a unlikely mix of R&B, hip-hop, house, and disco, an odd hybrid that's become wildly popular, spawning stars like Bongo Maffin and the late Brenda Fassie. Much of the old center still holds, though; Ladysmith Black Mambazo and the Mahotella Queens (now without Mahlathini, who died in 1999) have both ascended to international world music superstardom, and groups like the Soul Brothers are still going strong.

South Africa developed a jazz scene that was, obviously, heavily influenced by American jazz, especially the swing bands of the 1930s. From there it developed a more individual take on the music by adding elements of their own marabi music that took it in a different direction.

Probably the best-known name in South African jazz is trumpeter and vocalist Hugh Masekela, who started out in the 1950s with groups like African Jazz and the Merry Makers, before joining the Jazz Epistles. But there'd been a jazz scene, especially around Johannesburg, since the 1930s. Masekela would move to the United States to escape Apartheid and study in New York, finding real success in 1968 with the hit "Grazin' in the Grass" before returning to Africa in 1972 and residing in Ghana. After a move to Botswana, he headed to England, where the wrote the score to the musical *Sarafina!*, after which he hooked up with Paul Simon for his *Graceland* tour. With the end of Apartheid, Masekela was finally able to go home and has been making music in South Africa—and encouraging others—since. And in recent years, South African music has undergone a renaissance, with artists like the angelically voiced Vusi Mahlasela emerging.

Much South African jazz, especially the more avant-garde jazz, found an outlet in London, especially in the open musical scene of the 1960s, where saxophonist Dudu Pukwana and pianist Chris McGregor had a chance to shine with their band, Brotherhood of Breath.

Zimbabwe: South African mbaqanga is but one element in Zimbabwean jit, a music that also draws on Congolese rumba and the music of the local Shona people. It's music to dance to, popular music with rippling guitars and a strong beat, typified by the Four Brothers or the Bhundu Boys (who found popularity in the United Kingdom).

It's irresistible music and perfect for Saturday nights at the bar, where it remains popular, but it's not the heart and soul of Zimbabwe. That belongs to the mbira, or thumb piano. The instrument occurs in other places in Africa (most notably Tanzania) with other names. With metal keys and a sound-box to amplify the notes, it can create a hypnotic, otherworldly feel, especially when several of them are set up to play different parts that overlap. It's a sacred instrument, used in many ceremonies by the Shona, although it's made its way into secular music, too. Stella Chiweshe combines both aspects of the instrument, playing and singing to create highly spiritual music, as did the late Ephat Mujuru.

The mbira is also at the center of the sound of Zimbabwe's best-known musical export, Thomas Mapfumo. With his flowing dreadlocks, the chimurenga (struggle) music, played by his band, Blacks Unlimited, was the soundtrack of the war that liberated Zimbabwe—formerly Rhodesia—in the late 1970s. At the time, ironically, the mbira lines weren't played on the instrument itself but replicated on electric guitars; Mapfumo didn't bring real mbiras into the group until 1987. During the late 1980s and into the 1990s his growing criticism of corruption and incompetence in the Mugabe regime made him unpopular with the government, to the extent that he now lives in exile in the United States.

Mapfumo's been a major attraction on the global world music circuit for a number of years now. While not yet as big internationally, Oliver Mtukudzi, known affectionately as "Tuku," has become more popular than Mapfumo at home—his *Tuku Music* was Zimbabwe's biggest-ever selling album. While there are touches of mbira in his music, he draws equally from jit, South African mbaganga, and even Western soul music. A very strong songwriter, he's had support from American Bonnie Raitt, who used one of his songs as the basis for her "What's Going On?" His last three albums have been released internationally, giving him wider exposure, which has been reinforced by several well-received tours. He seems poised for greater Western popularity.

Mozambique: Mozambique has been crippled by natural disasters, but somehow music has survived. The urban style called marrabenta (broken string) has remained popular, especially around the capital, Maputo. Euyphuro, a group that first recorded in the 1980s, but reconvened in the late 1990s, is one of the best exponents of the style. But their preeminence is now being challenged by Mabulu, a multigenerational band that can switch from old-style marrabenta to rap in a heartbeat. Marrabenta's oldest living star, Dilon Djindji, has also received more exposure since 2002 with the release of a solo album.

These are signs that Mozambique is slowly bouncing back, and that artists still have plenty to say. Encouragingly, the albums of all the mentioned artists are available in the West.

Tanzania: If there's just a trickle of music coming from Mozambique, there's even less from Tanzania, which barely has a recording industry these days (although a small label, Limitless Sky, is hoping to help change that). That doesn't mean, however, music isn't played; there's still a healthy amount of live music. It is interesting that some comes from Congolese artists who traversed the continent to make Tanzania's capital, Dar es Salaam, their home. And so the strains of Congolese rumba—slightly changed with the passage of time and sung in Swahili, but still recognizable—can be heard from musicians like Ndala Kasheba and the legendary Remmy Ongala, who's become one of Tanzania's biggest stars, a man who's constantly been outspoken in his lyrics, championing the poor and advocating the use of condoms to prevent the scourge of Africa, AIDS.

The country's musical icon, though, is the late Dr. Hukwe Zawose. Self-taught on the ilimba (the local name for the thumb piano) and the zeze fiddle, and blessed with a voice that can span several octaves, he specializes in the traditional music of his Wagogo people and other native tribes, in addition to writing his own, traditionally influenced material. He first achieved national success after being "discovered" by Prime Minister Dr. Julius Nyerere, and since then his legend has grown. For many years he was the leader of the country's National Music Ensemble, and his albums for Peter Gabriel's Real World label (as well as his opening for Gabriel's tours and frequent WOMAD appearances) made him a magnificently talented staple on the world music scene.

There's yet another facet of Tanzanian music, one that's spread beyond the border, to the Muslims across East Africa— from Zanzibar to Kenya. Called taarab, its sound is vastly different from anything else in the area, with powerful Arabic inflections but also tantalizing hints of African and even Indian music. It's inviting and infectious, especially in the hands of a big band like Zanzibar's Culture Music Club, but it also works well in smaller ensembles. England's Globestyle label has released several taarab albums, offering a taste of the delights to be found.

Kenya: In the past few decades, the sound of Kenyan popular music has been benga, with its distinctive "dry," clean guitar sound. Kenyans have been in love with guitar for decades, developing it in different ethnic musics. However, it's ironic that Kenya's biggest name, singer Samba Mapangala, isn't from the country at all, but one of many Congolese musicians who moved from their homeland to make a living from music. Over the course of almost thirty years, Mapangala's music has taken on a very warm Kenyan groove, with more than a dash of soukous in the mix. But the presence of guitars, and some wonderful playing, is strongly in evidence throughout his work.

Someone keeping acoustic traditions alive is Ayub Ogada, who performs solo, accompanying his captivating voice with the nyatiti (a small harp that looks like a Greek lyre). There's a disarming simplicity to his work that masks an unearthly beauty.

Uganda: The influence of Congolese music was felt in Uganda. Along with covers of European sounds, local bands played the rumba. But that was largely because there was little in the way of a Ugandan tradition from which they could pull.

There's an irony to the fact that the preeminent Ugandan on the world music scene had to flee the country in the trunk of a car during the Idi Amin years. Geoffrey Oryema was just a child then, but the sounds he'd heard in his formative years were the inspiration for his debut, *Exile,* on which his hypnotic, lulling voice plays above Ugandan melodies and rhythms. Since then his outlook has become more global, and while his singing remains excellent, much of the music has descended to a vague, transnational blandness.

The wandering minstrel tradition has remained strong around the capital, Kampala, where bar patrons can pay musicians to compose a song on the spot. Known as kadongo kamu (only a small guitar), it reached the world music scene through the work of the late Bernard Kabanda, whose sole CD, *Olugendo,* remains a joy and an insight into the world of Ugandan beer joints.

Madagascar: While the music scene in much of East Africa has mostly been static or declining, the huge island of Madagascar, known as "Big Red," has thrived—although recent political instabilities leave the future somewhat uncertain. Its polyglot population—the earliest settlers arrived from Indonesia, but over the years African, Arab, and French colonizers have added to the mix—and relative isolation in the Indian Ocean have made it a hothouse in which the music has developed in a unique fashion, taking on the colors of different groups while developing an individual style. Even the main instruments are definitely of the island—the valiha and marovany zithers (the valiha is tubular, made from bamboo, and the marovany looks like a briefcase with strings on both sides), and the kabosy, which resembles a mutant guitar but uses partial frets.

Throughout the 1970s, the 6/8 rhythm called salegy was the great popular music, eminently danceable, and—as performed by artists like Jaojoby—utterly irresistible. Along with watcha watcha (similar to the benga of Kenya), salegy helped drive Malagasy popular music, when local 45s could sell like hotcakes.

But that happened in isolation. It wasn't until the 1990s, when the British Globestyle label released two compilations of the music from Big Red, and American guitarists David Lindley and Henry Kaiser had recorded there, that Madagascar became a viable international musical force.

1992's *A World Out of Time*, which featured the duo working with a range of Malagasy musicians, helped a number of artists began to find international outlets for their music. Accordion player Regis Gizavo and valiha wizard Justin Vali were among the beneficiaries. Tarika, however, the band that emerged from the similarly named Tarika Sammy, have claimed the brass ring as Madagascar's leading act.

Stunning guitarist D'Gary has also received widespread praise. He's developed his style from something rooted in the Indian Ocean to a unique and virtuosic creation that acknowledges his past but isn't limited by it.

Ethiopia: For most people, the lasting image of Ethiopia comes from the mid-1980s, with its pictures of the famine that ravaged the country. Much has changed in the country since the fall of the Mengistu dictatorship in 1991, and a music scene has coalesced around Addis Ababa. Aster Aweke, one of the few Ethiopian singers to have an impact outside her native land, has long made her home in the United States, while keeping some of her roots fiercely alive in her music. Another up-and-coming diva, Gigi, who works in a more experimental vein, has also settled in America.

But it's the golden age of Ethiopian music, from the late 1960s and through the 1970s, that's caught the ears of world music fans. Buda Musique released a series of albums chronicling the fertile period, compiled by Frenchman Francis Falceto. While strongly influenced by American music, from soul to rock to jazz, the artists melded it with their own sounds, and the results are intriguing, both familiar and disorienting, not unlike wandering into a hall of mirrors. Much of the music is superb, like the disc featuring singer Mahmoud Ahmed, who was Ethiopia's Elvis, and the volume that focuses on the tezeta style, whose closest Western analogy is haunted, nighttime blues. But equally fascinating is the disc dedicated to Ethiopian jazz from the period. The ongoing series promises even more delights in the future.

Morocco: For many, Morocco conjures up misty images of the wandering 1950s beat writers, or the hippie trail of the 1960s. And it's true that the country did largely surface into Western consciousness then (although the film *Casablanca* made the name of the country familiar some years before).

But for many, their first tastes of Morocco came with the awkwardly titled *Brian Jones presents the Pipes of Pan at Jajouka*. Recorded by the late Rolling Stones guitarist, and enhanced with studio trickery to replicate his psychedelic experience of the time, it was the trance music of the Master Musicians of Jajouka. Using drums and pipes called ghaitas, they create a dark, unearthly sound that's completely timeless and primal. For almost a millennium these musicians made up Morocco's court orchestra, finally returning to their village in the Rif Mountains in the 1930s. Membership in the group still passes from father to son, as it has for almost a thousand years. And they remained lauded by Western musicians; jazz great Ornette Coleman has played with them, and they've been produced by American soundscaper Bill Laswell (who recorded them without studio effects) and Asian Underground pioneer Talvin Singh (who didn't).

In many ways, the Master Musicians are a brotherhood, similar to the Gnawa brotherhoods, whose ancestors were the slaves brought across the Sahara from West Africa and who also use trance music in their rituals. The Gnawa play their own distinctive instruments—small, castanet-like steel cymbals called garagab and the long-necked gimbri (also known as a sentir), which produces a resonant, throbbing bass sound. Expatriate Hassan Hakmoun, who now makes his home in the United States, is an accomplished gimbri player who's brought the instrument out of trance music to fuse it with other styles. Nass Marrakech also use the instrument as the basis of their sound, which, while more rooted, can be equally adventurous—as on their collaboration with Cuban pianist Omar Sosa.

The Gnawa element plays an important part in much Moroccan music (although they can also be found in Algeria). It's evident in the sound of Nass El-Ghiwane, for a long time of one North Africa's popular bands, who melded it with sha'bi for an interesting, lively fusion, and in the all-female B'net Marrakech, a group that breaks taboos, not only by being a female group but also by playing trance music, which has long been a strictly male preserve.

B'net Marrakech's impact has mostly been overseas, but a Berber singer who scored North African hits (her biggest being "Shouffi Rhirou" and "J'en Ai Marre" in the 1980s) was Najat Aatabou. Her very Berber sound owes more to the rhythms and feel of trance music than to Arabic music, although, like Nass El-Ghiwane, she's moved to a more sha'bi style.

The music of the Berber, or Imazighen, people is generally separate to most of the music of the Arab world, a signifier of the cultural and historical differences. Berbers live in Morocco, Algeria, Tunisia, and Libya and still actively practice their linguistic and musical traditions. The village music called ahwash, with its large choruses and call-and-response singing, and raiss, songs with oddly elliptical melodies sung by professional musicians—usually in more urban settings— both remain very active. Takfarinas, an Algerian Imazigh, has won some international acclaim for his Berber pop.

While raï can often be heard on the radio or blaring from cars, it's usually of the Algerian variety rather than any homegrown variant, as Morocco, perhaps surprisingly, has yet to produce any convincing raï. However, the country has come up with some excellent electronic and dance music, with artists like U-Cef and MoMo creating new hybrids that are rooted in the rhythms and instruments of the country, but bring in strong doses of the Western dance floor and the feel of tomorrow through loops and samples. Thanks to trailblazers like these, Morocco has become the center of the Maghrebi electronica movement called Arabesque.

Algeria: Raï isn't the only music to come out of Algeria (there's also the style called kabylia, which has updated traditional melodies of the Berber Kabylia people with Western instruments), but it's certainly the main one. Khaled, the King of Raï, is a superstar in world music. And Cheb Mami, now snapping at his heels, has also developed an international reputation.

The music's roots lie in the streets of Oran, a Mediterranean seaport in the west of the country. It evolved from the Bedouin milhûn poetry (closely related to Moroccan milhûn) of the middle class, accompanied by the guellal (a drum) and the gasba (a flute made of rosewood). But there were also working-class street poets, the zendanis, whose songs spoke more to the people, often interspersed with cries of "Ya raï" (*raï* translates roughly as "opinion").

Milhûn and the zendanis came together in the form of female singers, known as the cheikhas. In a country where females were supposed to remain largely invisible, these women were outspoken—and outcast from decent society. Their position and actions would make Madonna seem tame. The chiekha whose name stands out, partly because of her talent but also because of her visibility, is Cheikha Remitti (the nickname comes from the French word *remittez*). First recording in the 1950s, she made her reputation by a scandalous song that advised girls to lose their virginity. While much of her music has stuck close to raï's rural roots, in recent years some of her discs (notably *Sidi Mansour*) have experimented with technology and rock-raï fusion.

It wasn't until the 1960s, in the first heady days of independence, that musicians began their attempts to modernize raï. Trumpeter Bellemou Massaoud was one driving force, introducing brass and bass guitars to the sound, which let it compete with imported rock for the hearts of the young.

And the young did come, further transforming the music. By the 1980s the sound of raï had spread out of Oran and across Algeria; and a new generation of singers, such as Cheb

Khaled, Cheb Mami, and Cheba Fadela (*Cheb* and *Cheba* mean "young") were becoming known. Producer Rachid Ahmed was further revolutionizing the sound, using synthesizers and drum machines and ushering in the modern era of pop-raï, with its lyrics of rebellion and real life.

Khaled, as he became known in the 1990s, is raï's superstar, an icon within the genre who's made a global name. But Cheb Mami slowly found a global audience, and the music even began drawing from other ranks. Faudel, the young prince, was from an Algerian family, but born and raised in France.

Raï was the bedrock of a landmark concert in 1998, at which Khaled and Faudel were the headliners on the first all-Algerian bill at a major stadium in Paris—a sign that the *beurs* (as the Algerians are derisively called) had fully arrived. It was commemorated on the disc *1, 2, 3 Soleils*.

Also performing that night was Rachid Taha, an Algerian who'd grown up in France and been involved in the cut and thrust of punk rock. While not a raï singer, he melded rock and Arabic music into a raw, aggressive form, adding some dance beats and finding a receptive Western audience. But Taha stands as a musical law unto himself, a maverick, and unlikely ever to change. Raï itself, though, keeps going from strength to strength. Hopeful new artists constantly emerge, but in a field dominated by Khaled, Mami, and Faudel, few break out beyond Algeria itself.

Tunisia: For a country with a venerable history, Tunisia has never really developed a real music of its own. Instead it's always taken on outside influences, especially from Egypt and Algeria, along with the Bedouin of the South. The sha'bi street style, so prevalent in Egypt, has proved popular here, along with Arab classical music.

For several decades, Tunisia has been a place to leave

rather than to live. Like many Algerians, thousands of Tunisians have left their homes for the promise of a better future in Europe, most often France. But few have managed to make any mark musically, either abroad or at home. One of the few exceptions is the Paris-based female singer Amina. Representing her adopted homeland in the 1991 Eurovision Song Contest, she won with "Le Dernier Qui a Parlé," which daringly blended pop and African rhythms. Amina has been a relentless experimenter ever since, working with electronica pioneers Renegade Soundwave and recording a version of Billie Holiday's torch classic "My Man" that's pushed along by swooping Egyptian strings. In France she's been a star for more than a decade, but she's just beginning to find her feet on the international stage.

Egypt: In Cairo there's one thing for certain; walk down any street and people will be playing cassettes by the late, revered Um Kulthum, still regarded as the greatest singer Egypt has ever produced and a beacon of Arab classical music. But a younger generation is also likely to be playing the rawer sounds of sha'bi or the more pop-influenced jeel.

Like its Algerian cousin, raï, sha'bi began life as working-class street music, the voice of the people. As the years have passed, it's become a vital part of the Egyptian musical mainstream, growing more sophisticated in its approach, arrangements, and lyrics. At its best, however—as in the music of Hakim, who's risen to become one of the biggest stars on the scene—the rawness remains underneath it all. Songstress Natacha Atlas, who got her start with Britain's Transglobal Underground, has explored her Egyptian roots more and more in recent years, creating a type of music that owes debts to both sha'bi and electronica.

Amr Diab is, without any doubt, the big star of jeel. His

concerts sell out, and his cassettes (North Africa, like much of the world, is a cassette culture) sell in the millions. Although there's a definite slickness to his sound, there's also real personality in the songs—unlike, for example, so much of the plastic pop coming out of Lebanon. Curiously, he's yet to make any real impression outside the Arab countries, possibly because pop music doesn't easily transcend the language barrier.

Nubia, in the south of Egypt, was once a small but thriving country. However, the construction of the Aswan Dam meant that much of the population had to be forcibly relocated, and in the process much of an ancient culture was lost or at least started to disintegrate. Some, though, have tried to keep it alive. Hamza El Din, a master of the lute-like oud, an instrument common throughout the Middle East, has helped keep the flame burning on albums like *Escalay—The Water Wheel*. Another artist who made sure Nubia wasn't forgotten was Ali Hassan Kuban, who died in 2001. A multi-instrumentalist, he used the old rhythms, wedding them to both traditional and modern instruments for a music that was engaging and very soulful. Percussionist Mahmoud Fadl has taken it even further, both on his own and with his band, Salamat; while singer/songwriter Mohamed Mounir enjoys a more elegant, orchestral approach to Nubian music on his discs.

All of these artists have kept music vital, but the shining, lasting beacons of Egyptian music lie in the sphere of Arab classical music. It's an art in which words are every bit as important as music, and the lyrics truly are poetry. That's because poetry was seen as a high art in the Islamic world, bringing respectability to the more dubious (but still acceptable) music. Dating back as far as the eighth century, Arab classical music enjoyed a long period of fertility, followed by several more centuries during which it lay fallow, as Egypt came under the sphere of the Turkish Ottoman Empire. But in the early part of the twentieth century, it began to shine again, as Egypt started to reassert its national identity.

With the lyrics so vital, Arab classical music has always been a vocal art, and singers have become lauded, often not just in Egypt but also throughout the Arab world. In fact, it's often been the singers who have commissioned the songs, employing the poets and composers.

And many of the composers have become major figures in their own right during the past hundred years, often making huge contributions to the style. For example, Mohamed Abdel Wahab (who also made a name for himself as a singer and film star) helped modernize Egyptian music. He introduced Western elements and instruments (including electric guitar), and his music, such as "Cleopatra," caught the energetic essence of the "new" Egypt, as President Nasser moved the country into the modern, independent world.

But it was Wahab's partnership with singer Um Kulthum that was the crowning glory of his career, although he wrote for several other singers. Wahab and Kulthum enjoyed a long and fruitful association, and together they proved to be an unstoppable combination. Kulthum first came to prominence in the mid 1920s, and she rapidly became *the* major force in Egyptian music until her death in 1975. Her Thursday night concerts, first broadcast just in Egypt and eventually across the Middle East, brought the region to a standstill, and people gathered around their radios to hear her voice. There'd been no one like her before, and no one has yet equaled her.

The Middle East

Israel: As a young country, Israel is barely beginning to find its feet musically. There are many traditions from the Jewish Diaspora to draw on, but the nation seems to be trying to forge a new path. Violinist, oud player, and peace activist Yair Dalal is one who's helping the process by defining Israel's place in the Middle East, bringing a strong Bedouin influence to his music, in addition to other regional traditions. This coming together can make his work challenging—but it's also very rewarding.

The late Ofra Haza became a favorite in Israel for her pop music, but her impact on the West came after she recorded an album of Yemenite Jewish songs, all given a contemporary 1980s production. Called *50 Gates of Wisdom*, it was widely sampled and remixed, and made Haza into a minor known quantity and a relatively early world music star. Sadly, she died young.

Another woman, Chava Alverstein, has enjoyed a more sustained, if lower key, career. Her immediately identifiable influences are the female singer/songwriters of 1960s America, and for over three decades she's been performing with a very political bent to much of her material. In addition to her original work, she's also a longtime performer of old Yiddish songs and has even pushed at her own boundaries by successfully recording with an American klezmer group, strengthening the connection of the Jewish Diaspora.

Palestine: As there's not a deep Palestinian heritage, there's no real Palestinian music as such. And as Israel and Palestine are often reluctant neighbors, with strained political and economic circumstances, little has been heard internationally from Palestinian musicians. What has emerged on the West Bank in recent years, however, is some very angry hip-hop, as Palestinian teenagers vent their frustrations and ire through music. As yet, without much music business infrastructure, it hasn't really moved outside the country.

Almost the only Palestinian to have made an international

impact is oud and violin virtuoso Simon Shaheen. He's made traditional Arab music a vital part of his repertoire with his Near Eastern Music Ensemble, while exploring the more ambitious fusion of different styles of world music and jazz with his other group, Qantara. In addition he frequently lectures at schools and colleges and has gained respect as a composer of Western classical music, making him a man who can straddle several worlds.

Syria and Lebanon: In addition to folk melodies, which are still played in the old maqams, the great Syrian tradition is called muwashshah, a type of Sufi sung poetry that, perhaps surprisingly, can still have an effect on all ages and levels of the population. Perhaps the top living exponent of muwashshah is Sabah Fakhri, a remarkable singer in any estimation, and one who's remained dedicated to renewing the flame of the past. He's appeared and recorded with Lebanon's Wadi el-Safi, another venerable singer. But musically, Lebanon belongs not to a man but a woman, Fairuz, who won an eternal place in the hearts of all Lebanese when she refused to abandon her native Beirut, even at the height of the civil war.

However, while she's venerated, her music has been replaced among the young by the Lebanese pop style that's become generic, not only in the country but all across the Middle East. With light, frothy songs, mild dance beats, and relatively faceless singers, it's big business. Drawing heavily from Western pop ideas, but placing them in a Middle Eastern context, it's music that's meant to be quickly disposable.

Turkey: Turkey encompasses a cultural border, but it has far more in common musically with the Middle East than with Europe. The Turks share many of the same makams (maqams elsewhere in the Arab world); the scales, or modes of composition;

68 ▪ The NPR Curious Listener's Guide to World Music

and the idea of taksim (or taqsim) or improvisation, which allows instrumentalists to show their ability. The country has produced at least one great instrumentalist in the blind oud genius, Udi Hrant, who died in 1978 and whose breathtaking skills have been thankfully preserved on record. Along with Iraq's Munir Bashir, he remains the most important twentieth-century performer on the instrument.

The Romany people have a strong tradition in Turkey, and the reputation of clarinetist Mustafa Kandirali still towers above all others. However, the Istanbul Oriental Ensemble, lead by multifaceted percussionist Burhan Öçal, has become very visible in recent years, with its exciting, often gorgeous re-creations of Turkish and Thracian Gypsy music, both traditional and modern.

With its proximity to the Europe mainstream, a vital pop scene has grown up in Turkey. Alongside the usual lowest-common-denominator offerings, an accessible roots pop has grown up, embracing many elements of Turkish music for a satisfying sound.

Armenia: Armenian folk music has a deep history, as does Armenian sacred music, some of which dates back more than fifteen centuries. While the sacred music has stayed fairly pure, the folk music became part of a polyglot when Armenia was part of the Ottoman Empire, sharing several characteristics typical of the Middle East—the modalities and quarter tones, for example.

Armenians suffered greatly at the beginning of the twentieth century, most especially in the 1915 massacre by the Turks, an early attempt at ethnic cleansing that tried to wipe out the population. Many Armenians fled, often to America, where the majority made their homes in the California city of Fresno, and they took their music with them. Oudist Richard

Hagopian is emblematic of Armenians in general, maintaining the tradition as well as expanding it on his releases (issued by his son Harold on the Traditional Crossroads label, which specializes in music from throughout the region).

Not all Armenians fled, however, and their music has enjoyed a small renaissance in recent decades. Djivan Gasparyan, a master of the oboe-like duduk (Armenia's ancient instrument made of apricot wood) not only has taught at the conservatory there but also has become an international musical symbol for the country. He led a duduk quartet and recorded for Peter Gabriel's Real World label. At Real World, he undertook groundbreaking collaborations with guitarist/producer Michael Brook that have taken the instrument far outside its usual framework without ever losing the root of the duduk's majesty.

Iran: Like several other countries in the Middle East, Iran's great music heritage lies in its classical music, especially vocal music, which (like other Middle Eastern classical styles) places great emphasis on the words, often setting the words of major poets to music.

Until the end of the nineteenth century, though, classical music tended to be the sound of the aristocratic classes, reaching the masses only during the course of the past hundred years. It has a respectability (thanks to its poetic content) that evaded most music in a strongly Islamic society.

Of course, the country has undergone tumultuous change since the 1979 revolution, and the more Westernized ways of the past vanished. That meant that popular music, which had grown up in the more liberal times since mid-century, was banned. Googoosh, the diva who'd been the light of Iranian pop music for many years, could no longer record. It is surprising that she elected to remain in the country, staying silent, out of the spotlight and the studio. Just within the past few years, as things have eased politically, she's begun to tour outside the country's borders to sell-out crowds of expatriate fans, but she's yet to issue a new disc.

The new regime did encourage classical music, which was both a boon and an opportunity for a whole new generation of musicians. Singer Mohammad Reza Shajarian was already a star in 1979, having come to prominence at the start of the decade, and since then his star has continued to rise, until it's become the brightest in the country. Not only does he possess a remarkable voice, but his deep knowledge of Iranian poetry means he's a fount of knowledge within the classical music community. Most recently, he's been recording with other, equally talented individuals as the aptly named Masters of Persian Music, a kind of supergroup that looks set to burn brightly in the world music firmament.

Iraq: Iraq is the home of Arab classical music, where it's mentioned as far back as the eighth century. It eclipses any of the folk traditions, which have tended to be along ethnic rather than regional lines. The long tradition of classical music has been sustained for many centuries, and the Baghdad Institute of Music has earned a reputation as one of the greatest conservatories in the Middle East, training countless superb musicians. Until his death in 1997, oudist Munir Bashir was the apex of twentieth-century players to emerge from the country, without peer on the instrument, an unparalleled improviser, and master of the short, elegant phrase.

In the past fifteen years, Kazem Al-Saher, a graduate of the Baghdad Institute, has emerged as a major Iraqi figure, producing both pop and classical music.

An equally powerful tradition belongs to the Kurds, a people who inhabit Turkey, Iraq, and Iran but who remain essentially stateless. For centuries they've used songs as a means of oral history, not unlike the griots of West Africa, although there's no special singing caste. Not only are there big ballad-like songs but also family stories; everything is put into songs, which traditionally operate within a small melodic range and five possible rhythmic patterns.

Since the 1980s, the Kurds have largely lost what voice they possessed under the harsh regimes of their home countries. The music hasn't vanished, of course; it's simply disappeared underground, to rise again in the future, we hope.

Asia and the Pacific

For many Westerners, Asia remains the most mysterious continent. Indeed, culturally it extends beyond continental borders to include not only the giants of India and China but also Japan, Indonesia, Australia, New Zealand, and Hawaii. There's no single common thread that runs among and connects them all. Many of the cultures are ancient, with traditions dating back to well before the time of Christ. Others, such as India's Bollywood phenomenon, are relatively recent. It's an area where history and modern growth stand side by side, prosperity and abject poverty sitting as uneasy neighbors.

The old trade route known as the Silk Road aided the transfer of ideas and music between China and the Middle East, and it's quite possible to hear the exchange of influences as you trace the path of the route. Elsewhere in Asia, however, music has developed along lonelier paths.

Asia is home to some of the planet's most glorious music—the qawwali ecstasy of Nusrat Fateh Ali Khan, the truly unearthly overtone singing of Tuva, the heavenly gamelan music of Bali, and the slack-key guitar stylings that have grown up in Hawaii.

At its heart, music is an adventure, a leap into the unknown by the composers that pulls the listener along. And for a Westerner stumbling across Asian music for the first time, that leap becomes one of faith. Whereas the pentatonic scale that anchors so much of African music gives it a faint sense of familiarity, that's missing in a lot of Asian music.

We've become acquainted with several types of Asian music over the years—for many, the Beatles adding a sitar formed a gentle introduction to Indian music, so that nowadays it doesn't sound so "strange." The great voice of Khan can transcend any culture. The floating tones of gamelan or the chanting of Tibetan monks connects in a spiritual way. But the knotty problem of Chinese opera, for example, remains almost insoluble; to some it's completely unlistenable. Yet that can also be part of the joy of Asian music. Traveling without reference points, you're forced to take the music for what it is, not associating it with something closer to home or putting preconceptions on it; it has to be judged completely on its own terms.

While some parts of Asia were colonized by European powers, others remained free, and that's allowed a different kind of development to happen. China, after all, was a thriving civilization centuries before Europe, and that ancient tradition is reflected in some of its music. But even Indian classical music seems thoroughly free of the years of the Raj.

Starting in Australia, moving across the Pacific, and returning to work across the Asian mainland is a journey of surprises and many connections.

Australia: The Pacific Rim is a curious mix of new and old cultures. In Australia, the Aborigines were in the country for thousands of years before white people arrived, after which for many years they were treated as less than human. The ancient Aboriginal instrument is the didgeridoo (also spelled didjeridu), which musicians used as a way of communicating with the spirit world that they believe surrounds us all. Made from the hollowed-out limb of a eucalyptus tree (the wood is actually eaten out by termites) its dark, earthy tones reflect and imitate the sounds of nature. In the right hands, such as those of Mark Atkins, it can seem to go beyond sound to penetrate a deeper, primal level. However, the instrument has been co-opted by many musicians around the world (often from the New Age end of the spectrum) as merely another texture in their music, which has had the effect of devaluing it. To hear it in a proper context, then, can be a revelation, both exhilarating and disturbing.

For a moment, Aboriginal music did seem to stride into the modern age, with the band Yothu Yindi, which was briefly one of Australia's shining exports at the beginning of the 1990s. Their multicultural white and indigenous mix was strongly political, with one foot still in tradition and the other planted in rock. Their time in the spotlight was short, but they continue to ply their trade.

New Zealand: Until very recently, New Zealand has been very quiet on the world music scene. What music existed in the country was in small pockets, and there was no real concentration of Maori culture. The white settlers brought some folk music from their homelands, but it was certainly nothing cohesive. Finally, though, the country's music seems to be finding a voice—and it's not white. The Maori group Wai has begun to make an impact, and Te Vaka (who live in New Zealand, but come from the Pacific island of Tokelua) continue to garner praise for their political folk rock, with its base in the log drum rhythms endemic to many Pacific cultures. As yet, though, there's been no cohesive scene to emerge, although that might well change in the future.

Hawaii: Hawaii and the guitar seem inextricably linked, as if the instrument had always been a part of the islands' culture. But it was only during the nineteenth century that Mexican cowboys, brought there to work the ranches, introduced it to the islands. And the other instrument with strong Hawaiian associations, the ukulele, didn't arrive there until close to the end of the nineteenth century.

Before the arrival of Western missionaries, Hawaii had enjoyed a rich culture, which was largely destroyed—and many of their songs perished with it. The renaissance came with the guitar. The Hawaiian guitar was the first popular slide guitar style. Mississippi Delta blues had developed its own raw slide technique, but this was more mellifluous and melodic. Furthermore, the sound received widespread record release, not being categorized as "race" music and condemned to a musical ghetto. For much of the 1920s the sound was a craze, largely in America but also spreading around the globe. And the Hawaiian guitar would eventually lead to the development of the instrument most associated with country music—the pedal steel guitar.

But there was still another style, which had largely been confined to the islands. Fingerpicked on regular acoustic guitars, it was called slack key in honor of the different tunings involved—families of players would develop their own secret tunings and play either traditional melodies or write their own.

For many years it remained mostly local, unknown to the tourists, who lapped up the songs backed by ukulele, played at luaus, and accompanied by grass-skirted hula dancers. This was the music of Don Ho. But in the 1970s, the guitar began to emerge from its island shell, with the great Gabby Pahinui a leading figure. From that small starting point, slack key has grown, and now a second and even third generation of skilled players has emerged on the international scene. The music has largely been disseminated by the Dancing Cat label (founded by New Age icon George Winston, who's a long-time fan of the style). Pahinui's sons have followed in his footsteps as players, along with artists like Ledward Kaapana and Keola Beamer, even as the older generation that helped form the music slowly passes on. The younger players have brought other influences to bear on the music, ranging from jazzy touches to folk cadences; but slack key remains thoroughly Hawaiian. And these days, it's the trademark sound of the islands.

Polynesia: Polynesia covers much of the Pacific Ocean, made up of scattered groups of islands flung across the sea, seemingly at random. But if there's something that unifies them, it's the remarkable way they use the human voice—a mix of the way it's developed and also the hymn singing taught by zealous Christian missionaries who came to convert the natives (and for the most part succeeded) in the nineteenth century. Hearing the Tahitian Choir, for example, the influence of the church is apparent in the harmonies. But what the voices do with them has no precedent in liturgical (or Western) music. The microtonal dips and slides can sound genuinely eerie and alarming at first, as if the CD player is at fault. But once you accustom your ears to it, it's remarkably moving choral music.

Of course, different musics and dances exist all over the Pacific, but it's the voice that's the loudest instrument by far.

Japan: Perhaps it's not so strange that Japan, a country that's gone from trading on its past to living completely in the present and future, should no longer have a strong roots music tradition, preferring instead rapidly disposable pop music.

Some things, like the famed Kodo Ensemble drumming, remain alive and very vibrant. There's also a tradition of classical music, but it's become ceremonial, more a museum piece than anything vital. The old instruments—the shakahuchi flute, the shamisen lute, and the zither-like koto—are still played. But for the most part, Japan has gladly plunged headlong into Western culture at the expense of its past.

Except on the more remote island of Okinawa, that is. There the catalyst for the roots renaissance was Shoukichi Kina, the founder of Champluse, which played what's best described as roots pop, although he's since moved on to a rawer, more grounded sound. In his wake came several groups, such as the female Nenes. Their saccharine-sweet singing can be an acquired taste, but as the years have passed, they've moved outward from purely Okinawan music to embrace reggae and hip-hop, giving a global edge to their music (although that doesn't necessarily do it many favors).

Shamisen player Takashi Hirayasu is an alumnus of Champloose and a virtuoso on his instrument. He's become visible on the global scene via two collaborations with American slide player Bob Brozman, first with *Jin Jin/Firefly*, a 2000 exploration of Okinawa children's songs, then *Nankuru Naisa* a year later, which featured, among other delights, Hirayasu's own compositions. It's very appealing, and Brozman brings some Hawaiian influence in his playing that gels well with Okinawa for an acoustic Pacific treat.

Even the electronica/dance scene has discovered Okinawa, as two Americans going under the name Ryukyu Underground have mixed the island's traditional folk music with beats and loops, to a surprisingly strong effect, and have plans for even more rooted efforts in the future.

Indonesia: How do you describe the music of 13,600 islands, more than 3,000 of them inhabited and spread across thousands of miles? Even in an age of global communications,

Indonesia remains something of a backwater, home to hundreds of different ethnicities and languages. Gamelan is the ancient, hypnotic music of the archipelago, but, unsurprisingly, it's Indonesia's pop music that communicates across the cultures.

The influence of gamelan has been immense, reaching outside the Pacific to capture plenty of minds in the West. While it's a word that's often tossed around, few fully understand exactly what gamelan is. Looked at in exact terms, gamelan belongs mainly to Bali, Java, and Lombok, although variants of it exist all across Indonesia. And to clear up a frequent misconception, gamelan isn't a single instrument. It's actually the name given to an ensemble made up of tuned percussion instruments, metal xylophones (called metallaphones), gongs, and drums. Sometimes, though, gamelan groups can be augmented with flutes and even voices, all of which boils down to mean that gamelan can be many things to many people.

Java is famed for its royal court gamelan tradition, which is every bit as regal as its name. The ensemble of this style revolves mostly about the metallaphones, although it's the large bronze gongs (the biggest more than three feet in diameter) that understandably garner attention for both their size and their massive sound. There's a defined repertoire of court gamelan music, and the sounds are slow moving, stately, and contemplative—a very spiritual music, which is exactly what it's meant to be.

More familiar to Western ears is Balinese gamelan, an altogether different animal. While hardly raucous, it's certainly louder, with each instrument doubled up and the music consisting of elaborate, interlocking patterns that shift and move the music forward. There's also a quality peculiar to Balinese gamelan that's achieved by having the pair of instruments not tuned exactly to each other; this creates a special, strange kind of harmony.

Having been documented by Western musicologists since the 1940s, gamelan has acquired a number of international fans, and it's not uncommon to find Western gamelan orchestras attempting either the repertoire from Indonesia or newer works. Some composers, both Eastern and Western, have written especially for gamelan orchestras. The style has had an undisputed influence on many avant-garde composers, most especially the minimalists, who've been attracted to the slow shifts of melody and rhythm.

While there are several Indonesian pop styles, the one that's shown real staying power, crossing the archipelago with no sign of fading, is dangdut, with its distinctive rhythm of a low beat to close one bar, and a high one to begin the next. The melodies are often seductive and languorous, and the stars of dangdut are big all across Indonesia, names like Rhoma Irana and Evie Tamala. It's remarkably accessible, a lush but easy listening experience, although it's yet to find a Western audience—or, for that matter, any real Western release. Compared to earlier folk/pop styles, like kroncong and gambang kromong, it sounds positively Western. Gambang kromong, in particular, offers an eclectic (possibly even bizarre) mix of native, Western, and even Chinese instruments for a music unlike any other, with fleeting glimpses of jazz and gamelan among other less readily identifiable elements. It's intriguing, chaotic, and frequently baffling, but in its own way remarkably satisfying.

In Bandung, far from the Indonesian capital of Jakarta, the main music is jaipongan, which emerged from the revival of regional music in the 1960s and has in turn become an influence on national music. Like dangdut, it's not readily available in the West; there are good examples of the style on *So La Li*, made in Indonesia by Sabah Habas Mustapha—a former member of 3 Mustaphas 3—with the local Jugala All-Stars

(Mustapha, who's actually British and named Colin Bass, had previously enjoyed a major dangdut hit with his song "Denpasar Moon").

Really, there are so many musical styles and variations in Indonesia that chronicling them is a major task. As close as anyone has come is The Smithsonian Folkways Music of Indonesia series. Over the course of twenty CDs, musicologist Philip Yampolsky tried to chronicle it all—from rural folk traditions to pop music. Of particular interest is the last volume, *Guitars of Indonesia*, on which the familiar instrument takes on a range of colors, ranging from something that sounds eerily like an Appalachian ballad to music that could only be from Indonesia. Taking the guitar (and some local variants) as a reference point makes for increased accessibility.

India: The West has become familiar with Indian classical music, thanks to the long careers of master performers like Ravi Shankar and Zakir Hussain. However, the true picture of Indian music is a little more complex than it initially seems: There are actually two separate Indian classical traditions, north and south, which differ significantly. And there's also the popular music of the subcontinent, typified by the songs that make up the soundtrack of the incredibly popular Bollywood films, which has become a genre unto itself in recent decades.

What's generally considered to be Indian classical music is actually the northern, or Hindustani tradition. The southern, or Carnatic (also spelled Karnatic) tradition is in fact older, dating back to the time before outside elements, such as Afghani music, infiltrated the north and changed it. Carnatic music has remained firmly in the folk tradition of music played every day, part of the fabric of life. Hindustani music was elevated (to a degree paralleling Western classical music) to become the sound of the upper class, heard primarily in the courts and homes of the nobility.

The sitar, with its buzzing sympathetic strings, is probably the best known of Indian instruments, and Shankar the performer with whom it's indelibly associated. The patronage of the late George Harrison from the Beatles made him a recognizable global figure, but Harrison simply apprenticed with the best and realized that the sitar isn't an instrument to be mastered quickly. Its complexities can take a lifetime to learn, and Shankar is one who has learned them. An *ustad*, or master, Shankar is a brilliant technical player, and his interpretation of the ragas is second to none. However, in his own way, he's also been an innovator of style (his daughter, Anoushka Shankar, has begun to make an enviable reputation for herself as a sitarist while still in her late teens).

Although the history of the sitar dates back some eight hundred years, it's actually the descendant of another instrument still in use, the veena. But it's the sitar, along with the sarod, another plucked string instrument (brilliantly played in recent years by Ali Akbar Khan), and the sarangi, a kind of bowed fiddle, that have come to exemplify the melodies of Hindustani music. The rhythm comes from the unmistakable tabla, actually a pair of hand drums, whose heads are coated with a paste of iron filings. In the hands of a virtuoso like Hussain, the tabla can sing as eloquently as any instrument or the human voice.

Ragas are the familiar form of classical music, and occur in both Hindustani and Carnatic traditions, although each approaches them differently; the southern form is often drastically shorter. Ragas (a raga is created from a thaat, which is a sequence of seven notes in a specific order) operate within certain rules and structures and exist for different times of the day, each with a different feel. Theoretically, within the nine different categories of raga, there are more than 484 possible types. But since ten different thaats exist in Hindustani music, the possibilities for the raga expand to 4,840. (Carnatic music has seventy-two thaats, meaning there are well over 32,000 possible ragas.) However, in practice, there are just some 200 main ragas.

Rhythm is as important as melody, and the cycles of rhythms and beats are often mathematically complex, meaning that a percussion player not only has to be technically highly adept but also learned in all the possibilities. Even though ragas are tightly structured, and musicians are judged on their skills in that structure, there is also opportunity for improvisation, by which outstanding performers can shine in their explorations around the melody and the mood of the raga.

Carnatic ragas don't offer the same areas of improvisation, which is the main reason for their brevity, generally lasting six or seven minutes, as opposed to the twenty minutes (or frequently more) of their Hindustani counterparts. In part that's because Carnatic music has stayed closer to its roots as a folk music. But it also has strong spiritual associations, frequently played in temples, and is often used as accompaniment for sacred dancing.

The veena, rather than the sitar, remains the preeminent stringed instrument in Carnatic classical music, and the bansuri flute and the piercing, oboe-like nagaswaram are also prominent melody makers. Within the past hundred years, the violin, introduced by Europeans, has also become important. For rhythm, the tabla isn't part of the tradition; instead the tunable double-headed drum called the mridangam is a leading instrument, along with the ghatam, a tuned clay pot.

Innovation has been more apparent in Carnatic than Hindustani music. Recent years have seen the introduction of such instruments as clarinet and saxophone, while U. Srinivas, a child prodigy on mandolin, has made that a part of the new arsenal of sounds, thanks to his lightning-fast fingers and melodic ability.

Indian instrumental music holds sway in the imagination, but both north and south have strong vocal traditions. Hindustani music has dhrupad, an ancient devotional form that's quite demanding of listeners in its slow stateliness. Less intense, but still revered, is the lighter form called thumri. More popular still is the semiclassical style of ghazal, whose origins are in Persia. Ghazals are essentially love poems set to music and are quite readily accessible to the ear. Even Pakistan's great Nusrat Fateh Ali Khan, renowned for his sacred qawwali singing, recorded a number of ghazals.

Inevitably, there's a crossover between Hindustani and Carnatic vocal music, such as bhajan and tillana (called tarana in north India). But the forms change in the different styles, having developed along different lines across the centuries. And while Carnatic music doesn't have dhrupad, it does have the praise songs known as kriti, which don't occur elsewhere.

The British Raj ruled India for many years, and its ghost is still evident in the country. The Raj's true musical legacy, though, is an unlikely one—brass bands, which generally play at weddings. Rather than any resplendent military ensemble, Indian brass bands function as an extension of folk music, usually playing film hits of the past and present. In a nicely ironic touch, Indian brass music has even hit Britain in the wake of Indian immigrants, and the London-based, multicultural Bollywood Brass Band offers a fine example of the style.

Another Indian style that has crossed the ocean to blossom is bhangra. Originally a harvest celebration dance powered by the beat of the massive dhol drum, it's somehow grown into a transnational Indian pop style, with plenty of followers wherever Indians live. The acoustic instruments of village bhangra have long vanished, replaced by guitars, keyboards, and singers who are big stars in the genre. It's still dance music, albeit distinctly urban and modern rather than rural. Anglo-Indians, in particular, have adopted bhangra as a musical expression of the young, and the British-based Asian Underground scene partially evolved from it in the mid-1990s. Bhangra was the first music to give Asian youth, especially those in Britain, a music of their own that was cool and danceable, connected to tradition but also modern. It helped form their identity in a Western society.

But no Indian popular music can compete with Bollywood, the *filmi* songs of the country's massive movie industry. More than the story, acting, or cinematography, it's the songs that make or break a film. And the movies are churned out in a manner that makes Hollywood seem parsimonious. The Mumbai-based industry, nicknamed "Bollywood" (the name is also used for the music), keeps fresh, usually highly romanticized, products coming, and keeps making stars of its actors or actresses.

The thespians don't sing, however; they merely lip-synch. The vocals are the job of the all-important playback singers, some of whom have also become major stars in their own right, like Asha Bhosle and her sister, Lata Mangeshkar, who—on the sheer volume of their work—are two of the most-recorded people in the world.

In Bollywood films, the actors break into song on the slightest pretext, and each one is a major production number. The people who can come up with the catchy songs, the ones that keep audiences coming back, are always in demand—the best of them working constantly on one project or another. These music directors, as they're called, range from the lush melodicism of A. R. Rahman to the aural mayhem of Vijaya Anand.

Rahman has become India's best-known composer, with a reputation built on film scores and songs (*Zubeidaa* was a typically outstanding example). He piles melody on melody but always manages to stop short of overload, allowing elegant, memorable vocal lines to shimmer over the top. Subtle Indian sonorities underlie all his work, but the overall feeling is strongly international. Considering that he didn't pen his first score (for *Roja*) until 1992, his rise has been remarkably rapid. And he looks to go much further, having cowritten the successful musical *Bombay Dreams* with the ubiquitous Andrew Lloyd-Webber.

If Rahman represents what might be called the high, sophisticated end of *filmi*, then Anand, along with many others, occupies the kitsch corner. The vocal melodies are always strong—as they have to be for Bollywood—but the arrangements can verge on the ridiculous. It's not uncommon to have shades of heavy metal, synth pop, techno, and sitar and tabla cheek by jowl in the same song. Without doubt, it makes for fun listening, quite addictive in its own way, and this is the side of Bollywood that's generally been captured on recent compilations and the one that's attracted Western listeners through its novelty. But for all the apparent random Cuisinarting of musical elements, there's always a fierce intelligence behind it, manipulating the strings.

The mingling of Western and Eastern elements indicates the kind of cross-cultural fusions that have been happening between Indian and Western music since George Harrison first plucked a sitar on "Norwegian Wood." In many ways it's been most apparent in jazz, starting with John Coltrane's explorations on 1964's classic *A Love Supreme*. And British guitarist John McLaughlin has probably done more than anyone to bring Indian music and jazz together, primarily with his group Shakti, which existed for three short years in the 1970s. Over the course of just three albums they created some fiery music, with impressive members drawn from both the Hindustani and Carnatic traditions.

More recently, V. M. Bhatt has been creating quieter fusions, playing his own creation, the Mohan vina. He's recorded duet albums with several American musicians, including roots guitarist Ry Cooder and dobro player Jerry Douglas, and spread farther afield by collaborating with Palestinian-born oud player Simon Shaheen.

In the mid-1990s, however, a different kind of fusion was spreading. In Britain, electronica and dance music has blossomed in the wake of late 1980s techno and raves, to the point that it has become the soundtrack for a young generation. Starting in the early 1990s, Asians who'd grown up in Britain, always caught between two cultures, began to add something of themselves to the music, with samples of Indian singing and music against breakbeats or hip-hop rhythms (taking inspiration from a 1970s sitarist, Ananda Shankar, who set his instrument against rock and early electronics in stirring fashion). And so the Asian Underground was born, a number of diverse artists coming together from time to time at club nights and releasing their own discs. It all seemed to coalesce in the middle of the decade around young tabla prodigy Talvin Singh (whose résumé includes classical Indian performances and appearances with avant-rock diva Bjørk), who started his own nights at the London club Anokha. First documented on a 1997 compilation, the Asian Underground quickly grew. Singh released a celebrated album, *OK*, that was a sophisticated fusion of dance and Indian music. That brought commercial success, and for a few brief years, the music was everywhere. As the scene emerged overground in the late 1990s, it was renamed Asian Massive, and these days is part of the more mainstream electronica/dance scene.

But these artists all owed—and acknowledged—a big debt to Sheila Chandra, who'd first broken into the British charts in the early 1980s and who continues to experiment with her voice and her music. In 2002, she guested with electronic band Jakatta and was rewarded with a reprise of her first hit, "So Lonely."

Pakistan: Pakistan is essentially a modern political construct, created in 1947 along with Indian independence. In fact, there were originally two separated Pakistans (one is now Bangladesh), havens for the Islamic population, to prevent clashes with the Hindus.

And it's Islam that's at the heart of Pakistan's major musical export. Qawwali, Sufi devotional poetry set to music, dates back to the thirteenth century. Musically, it has ties to the light classical music of north India, but the centuries have made it into a genre all its own, intended to bring listeners closer to God, to create and share a state of spiritual ecstasy.

However, it's vastly different from, say, American gospel music. Qawwali students—and the career or vocation of qawwali is handed down in families, always on the male side—undergo years of training, learning classical music and the basic repertoire of the genre. Following that, they serve an apprenticeship as part of a group, or party, as they're usually called. Eventually, if the musicians possesses the talent and become sufficiently learned, they might become lead singers.

The most obvious instrument (besides voice—everyone sings) in a party is the harmonium, which states and reinforces the melody line of the song, while the dholak drum provides rhythm (increasingly joined these days by tabla).

However good a party, it's the lead singer who commands

attention, for the quality of his voice, his improvisations, and that beatific state he and his fellow musicians can instill in listeners. After all, this is devotional music, and it's meant to transport both the audience and the musicians.

The greatest qawwali singer of the twentieth century was undoubtedly Nusrat Fateh Ali Khan, who died in 1997. He was the equal of the greatest operatic tenor, capable of dizzying flights of vocal improvisation that moved audiences of all creeds and colors to another place. He already had an international reputation when he recorded his 1985 Paris concerts, which remain, perhaps, the greatest testament to his true art—for the art of any qawwali is always in live performance, captured in the moment and moved by it, rather than in the more sterile confines of the studio.

Khan began working with the Real World label, and the higher profile transformed him into a superstar on the world music scene. But Khan was never constrained by the tradition of his music; in fact he embraced the opportunity to break new ground. During his lifetime, Khan recorded literally hundreds of cassettes for the Pakistani market, and even in death he remains prolific, as material from the vaults still appears regularly.

It's inevitable that he'll cast a long shadow over qawwali. For many Westerners, he simply *was* the music; and taken on any terms, he was a towering figure and one of the greatest singers of any kind of music.

But that doesn't mean others haven't made their own contributions to the music, or won't make powerful marks on it in the future. The Sabri Brothers should be heard by anyone with an interest in qawwali; in their own way they have as much power as Khan and his party, if not the vocal virtuosity. Among a younger generation, two of Khan's nephews were anointed by him as his successors, and their Rizwan-Muazzam

Qawwali Group has already established itself as a force—and one willing to experiment as relentlessly as their uncle.

Tibet: Tibet continues to fascinate Westerners. There's righteous anger at its ongoing occupation by China, which has torn the country apart. But there's also a more romantic sensibility at work, the fictional idea of a Shangri-La in the Himalayas. But much of the lure of Tibet lies in it being the home and the spiritual center of Buddhism. And Buddhism has had a powerful influence on much of the music made in the country, especially the religious music, which is what has found the biggest Western audience.

The chanting of the Buddhist monks ranges from reciting the sutras to singing hymns, employing a full chorus and accompanied by drum and cymbals. However, it's the Tantric monks who've received most attention. Having fled to India following Chinese occupation of Tibet, they continue to make their ancient music, with its multitonal sound, called gyü-ke, that emphasizes the overtones and harmonics of the notes (there's a faint resemblance to Tuvan throat singing). The Gyuto Monks Tantric Choir is the most widely recorded example, championed by musicians like drummer Mickey Hart of the Grateful Dead on albums like *Freedom Chants from the Roof of the World*. There's a true spiritual depth to this meditative music, which has found favor with both world music and New Age fans as well as helped other Tibetan artists like Nawang Khechog.

Tibet also has secular music, of course, and Yungchen Llamo has been a recent success story. She escaped the country by traveling on foot over the Himalayas. Her debut album, *Tibet*, allowed her glorious voice to shine unaccompanied, while the follow-up framed it in subtle modern textures. She's become a favorite at festivals around the world, but, more important, she keeps awareness of Tibet and the political situation high.

Afghanistan: The Taliban did everything it could to silence music in Afghanistan. They smashed instruments when they found them and beat the musicians. Music was banned from radio and television. But making music seems to be part of being human and can never be destroyed entirely.

Historically, there are strong ties between Afghani and Hindustani classical music. Many of the ragas are the same, as are the ghazals, which can be found all across the Middle East and Central Asia. Some of the instruments are also related; for example, the Indian sarod descended from the Afghani rubab, a kind of plucked lute.

In spite of their several commonalties, Afghani music has never been recorded in the way (or amount) Indian music has been. However, Ustad Mohammad Omar, the great virtuoso of the rubab, was recorded in concert while a visiting artist at the University of Washington at Seattle in 1974, accompanied by Indian percussionist Zakir Hussain.

In folk music, there's no unified style for the country—each region has its own, but none is well documented. The traditions of both classical and folk music run deep in Afghanistan, and the interruption of the Taliban wasn't long enough to completely stop the flow. What will prove really interesting is what the country does with its music, having regained it.

Burma: Burma, or Myanmar, as it's known these days, is the country whose music has largely remained hidden. Nestled between China, Thailand, and India and taking on small flavors of each, it's stayed quite distinctive—if largely unrecorded. There does exist a classical repertoire of "great song," which are duets for voice and the unusual Burmese harp, some of which can be found on *Mahagitá: Harp and Vocal Music of Burma*. The biggest surprise in Burmese music is the appearance of the piano. Brought to the country by Westerners, native musicians play it in a more percussive style. Musicians have adapted local music to the instrument, in addition to composing new pieces, with melodic structures and harmonies that sound odd to Western ears but are still weirdly beautiful. *Sandaya: The Spellbinding Piano of Burma* offers a glimpse into this very specific little world.

Vietnam: Vietnam has co-opted elements from all its occupiers into its music. It is interesting that it's never been at the sacrifice of a true native feel; if anything, the other strands stand as coloration, hints of a long, venerable history.

One of the country's leading cultural exports has been its remarkable water puppetry, often accompanied by an ensemble similar to that used in the folk opera (or hat cheo) style. With strings plucked and bowed, percussion (including gongs), and flute, the musicians mix folk and traditional tunes, accompanying the action and musically commenting on it. The glissandos of some of the strings and the sharp sweetness of some of the melodies can be particularly affecting, especially the playing of the dan bau, an instrument that exists in no other country. It has only a single string stretched over a soundbox. One end of the string is attached to a horn which, when moved, can alter the string tension. Plucked at the harmonics, the instrument has a unique sound, not unlike the human voice but possibly far more flexible and astonishing.

It's perhaps not too surprising that there's stateliness to Vietnam's court music, both theatrical and ritual. The styles may not exemplify the music of the people per se, but they offer an insight into the old ruling classes.

As with most Asian countries, the roots of the music run very deep, sometimes several thousand years (indeed, the oldest discovered instrument is from Vietnam, a tuned stone xylophone). Song traditions like quan ho can still be heard in the countryside, while a more modernized version of folk music has found some favor in the cities.

Go into any Vietnamese restaurant anywhere on the planet, and the chances are you'll hear Vietnamese pop music playing in the background. It's largely faceless music, created with even more assembly-line skill than its Western counterpart. Sickly sweet at times, it seems to have two speeds—slow and fast—with no variation in between. Intended to be disposable, there's usually little that's memorable about the songs or the singers. It's the antithesis of the older styles but a comment, perhaps, on modern Vietnam.

China: To many Westerners, Chinese music can be the most daunting of all, most especially Chinese opera, with what sound like bizarre, deliberately strange dissonances. Chinese opera is perhaps as close to a single national music as the country gets. With origins dating back fully two thousand years, it's a form that's continued to develop and spread, with a history of widespread popularity behind it. Although different areas have developed their own forms, with specialized musical variations, all opera is very stylized (as, indeed, is Western opera). And it's that style that can be so off-putting to Western ears. Gorgeous to see, with spectacular costumes and action, it's quite percussive, while demanding that singers of both sexes perform in high-pitched voices that simultaneously manage to be guttural—a grating combination. Calling it an acquired taste is accurate, although few in the West persist long enough to acquire it.

However, don't stop at the opera. The real folk music of

China works in the more familiar pentatonic scale and, at its heart, is surprisingly simple, as each piece revolves around a single melody line, decorated and offered with variations by the musicians—in a way not a million miles from Celtic music.

Given the fact that China's such a vast country, and one with such an ancient history, it's inevitable that music will vary wildly from region to region. However, for the most part Chinese music is that of the Han people, who make up the vast majority of population (the minorities live out toward China's borders and have their own music). And it's from them that we gain our ideas of Chinese folk music and its instruments. It's worth remembering that long before Europe or Africa, China had developed a musical system and instruments.

One of the most revered of those instruments is the qin zither, which was being played six centuries before Christ and is still in active use today. Slow and meditative, it's as graceful as watching a tai chi master. The four-string, lute-like pipa is mentioned as far back as the second century B.C.E. and is still a major instrument in Chinese music. There's a vital continuity to the music and the sounds.

The predominant musical style in south China is sizhu, or silk and bamboo, which uses bamboo flutes along with plucked and bowed string instruments (the silk of the equation, as the strings were originally made of that material). It's a lyrical, expressive style that's gained the greatest exposure and acceptance in the West, with the pipa sometimes engagingly at the forefront. A virtuoso like Wu Man can use the instrument to evoke almost anything, from percussive sounds to lulling melodies.

While sizhu began as village ritual music, urbanization has made it into something far more secular (although the village rituals do persist). It's become the true folk music of the region, often played in public at teahouses. While the music does have some young followers, it's suffering much the same fate as folk music everywhere, becoming the province of the middle-aged and the old, as the young go for more modern sounds.

And like all folk styles, a world of music exists within sizhu. There are the slow tunes with aching or peaceful melodies, which contrast with faster pieces with more complex rhythms. Often the titles are the clue to the image within the music. And unlike many folk traditions, it's ensemble music, made for listening rather than dancing.

In northern China, on the other hand, the traditional music is based on reeds and drums. It's the home of the ancient sheng, an ancestor—albeit well removed—to the harmonica. The instrument is traditionally used at ceremonies.

The predominant sound throughout the countryside, however, is of the shawn (a double-reed, oboe-like instrument) players and drummers (chuigushou), who are heard at the ceremonies marking life passages—weddings and funerals. The musicians play everything from traditional and classical music to current hits; curiously, this same mix of reed and drum and musical styles can be found as far away as Greek Macedonia, where Romany musicians still make a living with a similar lineup (using the reeded zurna and drum and playing a repertoire of both traditional and contemporary material). And wherever variants of the reed instrument occur, it's a constant that they're played with circular breathing, allowing the musician to hold notes or keep playing indefinitely, with no pause to inhale.

Chuigushou is music made for people, to entertain and mark major events. Often played outdoors, it's a spectacle best seen as well as listened to, as entertaining to watch as it is to hear.

Perhaps inevitably, the tentacles of Western pop have reached China, mostly through Hong Kong (although, as more Chinese cities open up, that trickle is gradually becoming a flow). Until recently a British colony, Hong Kong has adapted the Western sounds into its own pop music, known as Cantopop (for the largely Cantonese-speaking population), with its own range of big stars. While it's insinuated itself into areas of the mainland, it's yet to make huge headway, although a strong electronica scene is reportedly growing in Shanghai.

The Chinese minorities tend to live on the fringes of the country, both economically and geographically. However, the term itself can be a little misleading; given the size of the Chinese population, a minority can still mean several million people. Being so far-flung, some of these provinces have a culture and music more associated with other peoples—in southwest China, for example, the music uses the same pentatonic scale as sizhu, but the main instruments are very different, being mostly gigantic, unlikely bamboo harmonicas called *lusheng*.

Most minorities, however, are in the northeastern provinces—where Manchu, Koreans, and Mongols live and keep their arts very much alive.

In northwest China, the influence of the Silk Road traders is still apparent, as the musicians play maqāms (or muqams) that are similar to those from Central Asia, and Islam remains a strong religion—in sharp contrast to the rest of the country.

The Silk Road (a term that originated in the nineteenth century) wasn't actually one road, or even *a* road, at all. It was a series of trade routes that connected China with the Middle East (and, by extension, with the Mediterranean and Europe).

Caravans headed in both directions across Asia. From the West they carried gold, jewels, and, in the early centuries of the route (which dates back over two thousand years), glass. Heading West came furs, bronze, and jade—and, of course, silk. The music traveled in both directions, spread by the travelers.

Recently, the Silk Road Project has actively followed the music of the Silk Road. The CDs not only point out how the music traveled and influenced other music—in both directions—but also have spurred the commission of new work from composers living in Silk Road regions. *The Silk Road: A Musical Caravan* offers acute insights into how the cultural exchanges worked and their effects, made all too apparent by the musical illustrations. *Silk Road Journeys: When Strangers Meet* comes from the Silk Road Ensemble, under the artistic directorship of celebrated classical cellist Yo-Yo Ma. The disc includes both traditional pieces and new compositions. The two albums offer complementary sides of the same coin, the first being field recordings, the second the work of some of the world's greatest instrumentalists, often playing non-Western instruments, such as the duduk or the pipa. Both are equally powerful.

Mongolia and Tuva: In many ways, it's almost impossible to distinguish between Mongolia and Tuva. There are geographic borders, of course, but the two countries share so much and are carved out of the same central Asian steppes. For both, it's the rhythm of horses, for centuries the main form of transport, that informs and underlies their music. Under Communism, there were many attempts to eradicate the old cultural ways, but the relative isolation and decentralization of the area helped ensure they will never vanished completely.

As in other countries, the traditions have heavily rebounded. There are the old instruments, such as the horse-head fiddle—whose strings are still made from horse hair—and the spike fiddle. But, more than anything else, the music that's become associated with the region, especially with Tuva (although it also occurs in Mongolia), is overtone, or throat, singing.

Similar to the chanting of the Tantric Buddhist monks of Tibet, throat singing allows a performer to simultaneously produce two or three notes by emphasizing the harmonics. The sung melodies are actually from the modulations of the harmonics. Over the centuries, several different styles of throat singing have developed—kargyraa, for example, resonates around a deep bass, while sygyt offers a sound that's almost flute-like. First heard in the West through the field recordings on *Tuva: Voices from the Center of Asia*, throat singing has beguiled Western audiences.

To hear it, especially in concert, is a remarkable experience, an understanding of what is possible with the human voice. Over the course of a decade, the Tuvan group Huun-Huur-Tu has become the brand name in throat singing, releasing several albums of traditional and contemporary music. They perform folk songs of the region in addition to their vocal acrobatics of throat singing, and the horse theme, endemic to central Asia, recurs throughout their work.

But they're not the only singers around by any means. Kongar-ol Ondar has made an international name for himself, and Albert Kuvezin, one of the original members of Huun-Huur-Tu, has formed Yat-Kha, a much more electric, modern group. However, there's still plenty of the old style to be found in their music.

While it's generally a male preserve, one Tuvan woman has gained renown as a singer. But Sainkho Namchylak is better known in avant-garde circles than in world music. Sounding like a cross between Yoko Ono and Bjørk, her music can be entrancing and terrifying—often within the same song. She employs overtone signing at times, but uses it sparingly.

Few Westerners have mastered the technique of throat singing. One who has is Paul Pena, a blind blues singer from San Francisco (his biggest claim to success was writing "Jet Airliner," which became a hit for Steve Miller in the 1970s). First encountering throat singing on the radio, he tracked down a compilation and, through trial and error, managed to teach himself the technique.

The Academy Award–nominated film, *Genghis Blues*, traces Pena's involvement with throat singing. After demonstrating what he'd learned to Kongar-ol Ondar at a Bay Area concert, Ondar invited Pena to Tuva to take part in a throat-singing competition—the very first time any Westerner had participated.

Ondar and Pena developed a bond during Pena's stay in Tuva, sharing more than formalities as Ondar gave the American party a tour of the country and even invited them into his home. With his bone-rattling kargyraa, Pena—whom the locals nickname "Earthquake"—won a prize; he treated competition-goers to a largely impromptu concert that mixed throat singing and blues in an easy, natural fashion.

Although Pena was the focus of *Genghis Blues*, the film also offered insights into the nature of throat singing, both as art and politics, and provided glimpses of a country few outside Asia are ever likely to see. Perhaps more important, it gives an understanding of throat singing, and a very human portrait of both Ondar and the complex, shifting figure of Pena.

Azerbaijan, Uzbekistan, Kazakhstan, Tajikistan, Turkmenistan, and Kyrgystan: The republics of Azerbaijan, Uzbekistan, Kazakhstan, Tajikistan, Turkmenistan, and Kyrgystan might seem like obscure dots on the map or names from tiny items on the news, but together they cover a vast geographical area and a range of cultures. The westernmost of the countries, Azerbaijan, reflects its geographical position in its music, where the mugam (very similar to the Arabic maqām) holds sway—although that can also be found reflected farther east. The instruments, too, are similar to those found in Iraq and Iran. But the country's star performer isn't an instrumentalist. Alim Qasimov has developed a well-deserved international reputation as a singer of the mugams. Not only does he possess a remarkable technique, but the way he works around the music—with not so much improvisation as ornamentation—has helped set him apart from so many singers, majestic and masterful.

Uzbekistan seems to be having success with female singers, as both Yulduz Usmanova (who's been a popular performer for more than a decade) and Sevara Nazarkhan (a relative newcomer) have caused some ripples with their appearances and CDs. They are, however, at the pop rather than the traditional end of the spectrum.

Turkmenistan's Ashkhabad specialize in wedding music (always an infectious, upbeat style, no matter where it originates) and have expanded the possibilities of their sound by bringing Western instruments into the ensemble, alongside the more traditional dutar and serp. They've also collaborated with artists from outside their homeland, such as Greece's Melina Kana.

Europe

For all that the Old World seems relatively stable, the forces of history have caused plenty of turbulence over time. The Celts emerged at the end of the Roman era (about 400 C.E.) to be a dominant force for a few hundred years, only to be pushed farther westward by successive tribes. They now occupy the very fringes of Europe. When Islam was at its height, Spain virtually became an Arab country, and many of the traditions from that time still influence Spanish music. Religious and political persecution of all kinds has sent people looking for new homes in other countries for centuries. Populations are fluid, and the music they bring with them has an inevitable influence on local tradition.

Even as the European nations currently attempt to forge a single political unit with the European Union, they're also examining their own identities as the new century begins. For many of them, those identities are rooted in the past—frequently the colonial past. But the new multicultural societies that have emerged mean a long period of self-examination and soul searching to understand exactly what it means today to be "from" any particular country.

But the musical hybrids that have emerged from this can be thrillingly vibrant and indicative of a way forward. France has done a particularly good job here, with several bands seamlessly blending the music of a number of cultures to create something completely fresh.

Other countries have created something new out of the past. This has been particularly evident in Nordic music, in which a young generation (many of whom have been schooled in folk music at the college level) has reinvented folk music to make its sound relevant again. But reinvention is the very nature of the folk process and what stops the songs and tunes from becoming more than the quaint curiosities of a museum.

Where there's been oppression—in countries like Romania and Russia—music is just beginning to find its feet again. Not that it ever went away, but what was "state sanctioned" and what was "of the people" were often two different things.

In Europe, more than any other continent, we can trace

a continuous history of the music because people have been collecting it for over a century. And some families, like the Coppers of Sussex, England, have records of songs that go back much further. The Industrial Revolution urbanized Europe to a remarkable degree, drawing rural populations to the newly burgeoning cities, which brought together different regional traditions into a new melting pot. And out of that emerged a new music with a more cosmopolitan style and sophistication.

The surprising thing, perhaps, is that the rural traditions have lasted into an age of mechanization, mass communications, and global warfare. But we should be grateful that they have, for without them the roots of European music would be sadly lacking. And if, as they say, you can understand the future only by understanding the past, then those traditions are especially vital.

An apt place to begin is Russia. Perhaps more than any other European country, it's undergone several reinventions in the past century, and its sheer size brings it close to Asia— a connecting point between two cultures.

Russia: The largest country in Europe stretches from Asia to the Baltic Sea, and from the freezing Arctic down to the Middle East and the warm waters of the Black Sea, almost within reach of the Mediterranean. It's been ruled by czars and communists and has been a feudal empire and a socialist utopia. What was once the mighty U.S.S.R. has splintered into a number of countries since the fall of Communism, and the evil specter of the Eastern Bloc has been consigned to the history books.

Communism purged virtually all of Russia's musical past. Folk music was organized in rural areas by "folklore collectives," in which nonapproved material was not allowed (although a fair amount survived underground). Even the collective farms spawned their own songs, creating a new type of folk song. And those artists who gained state approval played music whose lyrics were heavily censored and all too often gray in arrangements and presentation. Few of the old traditions were allowed to remain, although some of the Cossack melodies stayed intact, almost as showcases of Russian folk music.

Since the fall of communism, the country has been struggling to find itself and forms of expression. It's not simply a case of developing something new but also of rediscovering the past.

Russia's foremost folk musician is the classically trained Sergei Starostin, who's come to specialize in playing various folk flutes and horns as part of the Moscow Art Trio and of the folk/rock band Farlanders, where's he's teamed with singer Inna Zhelaniya. He doesn't so much keep the past alive as place it in a new context and open up the rural past for all Russians to see. A student of folk music since 1977, he's traveled extensively within the massive country, learning different regional traditions.

The Terem Quartet combine folk and classical music in their act and play it all in manic fashion. While their original idea might have been to spoof the huge balalaika (an indigenous Russian stringed instrument) orchestras that were portrayed as the essence of Soviet folk music, they've taken on a life of their own. Three balalaikas (including the gigantic bass) and an accordion play Russian music at hyperspeed—and with great glee. It's more enjoyable in live performance, but their albums are a sly pleasure, too.

But the biggest Russian star has his roots not in folk or in classical music; he comes from rock. Boris Grebenshikov first came to prominence during Communism with his underground band Aquarium and is still a part of the group. But for almost twenty years he's maintained a solo career, which has looked more closely at Russian styles—the equivalent, more or less, of an American singer/songwriter delving into old country and blues with his or her music. While few of his albums have found international release, his reputation has traveled abroad, especially since Glasnost gave him an official voice.

Estonia, Latvia, Lithuania, and Ukraine: Like Russia, the music of the Baltic States suffered under communism, as Stalin attempted to create his brave new world. However, neither he nor his successors were able to completely eradicate the folk forms, which varied from country to country. And since independence, folk music has flourished in Estonia, Latvia, and Lithuania.

The Estonians share a tradition of runo-song with Finland. The runo-song itself is made up of short phrases, usually unrhymed; and for many centuries it was the preeminent Estonian folk form. Only around a hundred years ago did a more generalized folk form appear, with rhyming stanzas and full instrumental accompaniment. Kirile Loo is an artist who's kept the Estonian runo-song tradition alive on her discs, adding samples to the traditional instruments of her musicians.

Latvia also has a tradition of short unrhymed songs, somewhat similar to runo-songs, called dainas. The singing style has long revolved around a drone, while the main accompanying instrument, for many centuries, was the zither, which occurs in different forms across the region.

The band Ilgi carried the banner for folk music through the Soviet years, despite plenty of harassment from the KGB. In the decade-plus of freedom, they've developed an international touring schedule, which includes the United States.

The group continues not only to record but also to educate the younger generation in Latvian folk music and folklore. Instead of the purely traditional music they once performed, they've begun writing their own "post folklore" material, as they term it.

Perhaps it's ironic that the music of Ukraine is most familiar because of musicians who've come from the country's diaspora; or it might be a comment on how effectively the Soviets dismantled the country's heritage. Historically, there are similarities with the music of Romania, most obviously in the strong village band tradition. But the main sound has always been vocal, especially choral, somewhat similar to the polyphonic female choirs of Bulgaria.

Plenty of Ukrainians immigrated to the United States and Canada and have tried to retain strong links with their past through various Ukrainian associations. Violinist Pavlo Humeniuk, the self-styled "King of the Ukrainian Fiddlers" was one such, and he recorded his fiery "village-style" playing extensively between 1925 and 1965.

But Britain was also a destination of choice. A sizable and active Ukrainian community sprang up around the industrial northern city of Leeds. The Ukrainians, led by Pete Solowka, are all descended from Ukrainian immigrants. They began in 1989 as an offshoot of the indie rock band The Wedding Present, before gaining their own separate identity. Over the course of several albums, the group has played traditional and contemporary Ukrainian music (as well as some British punk and post-punk tunes with translated lyrics) in a style that has its roots in their spiritual homeland, but is also injected with all the fire of rock.

Finland: Like many of the Nordic countries, Finland experienced a renaissance of its folk traditions in the 1980s, since which time they've blossomed, and made international stars out of acts like Värttinä, JPP, Gjallarhorn, and several others. Much of the credit goes to the Sibelius Academy in Helsinki, which in 1983 set up a folk music department, offering degree courses in the style. That's brought in young musicians who've learned the traditions and absorbed them as part of their own music.

At the heart of Finnish song is runo-song, which works lyrically in an alliterative manner, with the stress on four of the eight syllables of each line. Many of the epics of old runo-song were collected in *Kalevala*, published in the nineteenth century, and which came, as the Finns claimed, to represent the country's soul.

While Finnish music has adopted many Western instruments over the past two centuries, it adds one of its own to the arsenal—the kantele. Essentially a type of zither, it can have from five to fifteen strings. Recent years have seen players like Minna Raskinen take the kantele out of the purely folk domain and experiment with the possibilities of the instrument, to excellent effect.

The kantele no longer features in the lineup of Värttinä, but runo-song does. The female-led group has the form as an integral part of its sound, along with Finno-Ugric influences from the Karelia area, and women's singing traditions from Setuland, Mariland, and Ingria—and with multiple singers, the music is inevitably vocal. Formed in 1983, they've managed to achieve that next level without compromising their original ideals, and these days their own music and songs, seamlessly integrated with the traditional material, form a vital part of their repertoire.

While Värttinä is virtually a brand name in Finnish music these days, they're merely one of the most visible facets of the Finnish folk renaissance. With its four fiddles, JPP has been at the forefront of the string revival, showing a revitalized role for the violin in Finnish music. Gjallarhorn has looked outside strictly traditional instrumentation to include African percussion and didgeridoo. While folk music was their starting point, they've become adventurous in their sound, bringing in avant-garde elements that mesh surprisingly well.

The Sami people (formerly known as the Lapps) are, strictly speaking, stateless. But they inhabit the inhospitable territory that runs from northern Norway across into Russia, some of it covering Finland. Their music differs greatly from all other Nordic folk styles—in fact, it has much more in common with Native American music in the way the voice and drumbeat is used. And, given the idea that the first inhabitants of North America crossed a land bridge from northern Russia to Alaska, the connection seems plausible.

The core of Sami music is the joik, an improvised, impressionistic song that can describe actions, thoughts, or places—in fact almost anything. It's an art that depends almost solely on the voice, a necessity for nomadic people. While it's died out in some areas, a few people are keeping it alive, and Sami culture is slowly experiencing a rebirth and acceptance. Wimme Sari, known professionally simply as Wimme, has become one of Finland's leading joikers; his songs use adventurous music settings, ranging from unaccompanied to techno and New Age. Mari Boine might be less obviously infused with the joik, but there's a similar sensibility to her music. She's become a shamanistic figure and a cultural icon to the Sami people.

One instrument that's found particular favor in Finland is the accordion, especially the larger piano accordions, mostly because of the curious Finnish affinity for the Argentinean tango. To Finns, it seemed incredibly exotic, music that oozed sensuality and warmth. That may help explain why they took to it in large numbers, to the point that the tango has become a part of Finnish culture—more so than anywhere except Argentina. There have been plenty of Finnish tango songs, as well as musicians who've become stars within the genre, such as Eino Grön. The form has remained very simple, with accordion taking the lead instrumental role (as opposed to the smaller bandoneon of Argentinean music). While the passing years have made it into more of a middle-of-the-road style, with not much appeal to the young, it's remained popular; there's even an annual tango festival.

Although she doesn't play tango, Maria Kalaniemi is perhaps the most respected accordionist in Finland, covering genres from classical to folk/jazz fusions in her work. Also much lauded, but far more experimental, is Kimmo Pohjonen. Using a range of effects pedals and techniques, he takes the accordion to places it's never been before—even managing convincing accordion techno! A highly skilled and very imaginative player, he's out on the edge of music.

Sweden: Like Finland, Sweden has benefited by having college courses in folk and traditional music (at the Royal Academy of Music in Stockholm). It's brought forth a vibrant, educated new generation of players, like the members of Ranarim, who have plenty to offer music and the energy to change it.

However, it's only in very recent years that Sweden's own music has received academic recognition. But well before then, there was already a healthy folk music scene in the country, which had begun in the late 1960s and really blossomed during the 1980s.

The revival had been in instrumental music, which has always been the core of the Swedish tradition, centered on the national dance, the polska. While the fiddle was the main instrument, there was also a resurgence of interest in the unusual nyckelharpa, or keyed fiddle, a particularly Swedish instrument.

It's possible to find recordings of Swedish fiddlers from the early twentieth century, many of them great musicians who advanced the tradition and mostly playing in different regional styles. But the Swedish bagpipes were also an important folk instrument, and the voice was, perhaps, more important than them all. Vocals are used for the ancient ballads that date back to the Middle Ages and the piercing cow calls that can shatter any composure.

However, it was the 1980s revival that made folk styles respectable to the young, and the first bands to have much impact were Filarfolket and Groupa. They both brought in new elements—Filarfolket played a kind of folk/rock, whereas Groupa (which stills exists) blazed new folk trails in their unusual combinations of instruments.

It was in the 1990s that the full fruits of the previous decades could really be seen. A new generation of bands emerged, using technological advances alongside the old instruments, often to startling effect. Garmarna and Hedningarna were at the forefront, adding plenty of samples and making full use of vocals. Garmarna's Emma Hardelin is a particularly effective and compelling singer. Hedningarna have veered between the wild edge of technologically augmented music and a purely acoustic sound and appear quite comfortable with both.

The quartet Väsen is totally acoustic, and its playful approach to traditional and original music has won many fans. The group's nyckelharpa player, Olov Johansson, is one of the best in the world and has also worked with such luminaries as the Kronos Quartet.

Filarfolket's folk/rock lives in spirit with bands like Hoven Droven, who adds more than a touch of heavy metal to their polska (all the players are also accomplished traditional musicians), and Den Fule, who bring saxes and flutes to their rock-heavy approach. While an unlikely combination for Swedish music, it goes to prove the elasticity of the form.

It's only within the past four of five years that the folk graduates of the academy have begun to make a mark on the scene. Ranarim, made up of two males and two females, have kept to the acoustic path, whereas the instrumental fiddle duo of Harv (who have now added other instruments to their ranks) collected older tunes for their albums, alongside original work.

The folk scene is very open, in part because it's so compact. It's not unusual for someone to play with two or even three bands to air different facets of his or her personalities and to gain the experience of playing with different sets of musicians. It's something seen in other parts of Europe among young folk performers (Britain is another prime example). The effect is good, with people constantly bringing new ideas into their own music and pushing the folk process along.

Swedish folk music has developed rapidly and it continues to grow apace. Young people keep coming in and refreshing it, which ensures its vitality for the future. And the players of the 1960s and 1980s, who have been the great influences, are still active, giving a strong continuity to the field.

Along with Finnish music, the sound of new Swedish folk has found particular acceptance in the United States. In part that's because America has a good proportion of citizens of Nordic descent, who are proud of their heritage and eager to embrace it. Availability of the music has also helped; the independent Northside label dedicated itself solely to Nordic music. Many of the acts have toured, and together the three factors have worked to make Nordic music very visible in America.

Norway: There is a wealth of Norwegian folk music, both vocal ballads and instrumental music, some of which is played on the national instrument, the hardingfele, although it was traditionally played in the west of Norway (the regular violin had the eastern territory). Looking remarkably like a ordinary violin (although often highly decorated), what sets a hardingfele apart is the addition of four or five "sympathetic" strings under the fingerboard and bridge, which resonate when the instrument is played. Much of the instrument's repertoire is dance music, dating from the days when it was used as the instrument for dances, such as the halling, in rural regions. Probably the leading exponent of hardingfele today (although equally competent on regular fiddle) is Annbjørg Lien. Although she plays traditional music, she's not limited by it. In fact, her albums have shown a penchant for progressive rock and several other styles, but the root of her playing is utterly Norwegian.

It is perhaps surprising that Norway doesn't have as strong a roots music scene as either Finland or Sweden. It doesn't offer any formal education in folk music, which may have had some effect on that situation, because young people haven't been led to or trained in the music.

Denmark: Two centuries ago, Denmark was the dominant Nordic power, ruling much of the region, as far away as Greenland. These days, the country of Hans Christian Anderson controls only the Faroe Isles, out in the North Atlantic. The traditions of fiddle dance music and ballad singing—some of the epic Danish ballads date back several centuries—fell by the wayside in the early part of the twentieth century. The Danish government has a folk music department, which now actively encourages roots music, and, indeed, it issues an annual compilation of this music. However, Danish artists are beginning to make a mark internationally. The group Sorten Muld, who takes traditional ballads and reimagines them with a mix of electronic and acoustic instruments, has found a small measure of international recognition, while groups like Lang Linken, Haugaard and Høirop, Serras, and a crop of youngsters continue to push traditional music at home and abroad.

Scotland: Just a short journey across the North Sea from Denmark lies Scotland. One of the Celtic countries, it's experienced the revitalization of culture that began in the 1960s with the folk revival and has continued with political independence from England. Before that, the image of Scots music was kilts, bagpipes, and reels, which hardly did justice to the rich music and song tradition that had built over a couple of centuries, in spite of oppression.

The fiddle has become an important Scots folk instrument only in recent years. Before that, the song was the center of things, although it's the bagpipes that are forever associated with Scotland. In truth, they're not especially Scottish; in different forms they occur throughout Europe, and even on other continents. It's the pibroch, or big war pipes, that called the clans to battle, and which the tourists love. And the irony is, they rarely feature in Scots folk bands.

The dances, or ceilidhs, were once a regular feature of village life. Small groupings of musicians, often including a pianist, would play for the dancers. As more people moved to the cities, and the older ways started to die, the ceilidhs started to vanish. However, they have seen some revitalization at the hands of younger bands. Both the Peatbog Faeries and Shooglenifty have updated the tradition with some vibrant dance music that bonds the rave generation to the crofters. Multi-instrumentalist Martyn Bennett has gone one step further, adding some very hard techno to the mix.

The Gaelic element was vitally important in Scots song for many years and keeps a link to the country's past, which singers like Catherine-Ann MacPhee have kept alive. With the passing of time, however, fewer singers are using it, although Mouth Music adopted the peurt a beul singing (or mouth music) of the Shetland Isles on their first disc, a groundbreaking mix of Scots (Gaelic) song, African rhythms, and techno beats.

Although the old folk traditions were dying by the middle of the twentieth century, the folk revival of the 1960s brought more interest in the past. Everything gathered steam in the 1970s, as several influential bands were formed. The Boys of the Lough, the Battlefield Band, and the Tannahill Weavers all came into being then. The first group featured fiddler Aly Bain, one of the towering figures of Scots traditional music, and singer/guitarist Dick Gaughan. From performing traditional songs, Gaughan has gone on to become the country's foremost singer/songwriter and interpreter of material, a vital part of the folk scene.

Probably the most successful Scots bands are the ones who've taken the tradition and added something to it. Runrig, for example, began as a band playing ceilidh along with Gaelic songs. They revved up the rock element (and have also toned down the Gaelic), and now they fill concert halls wherever they play in Britain. Capercaillie also emerged from the traditional music scene, but in recent times have smoothed out their sound and edged nearer to New Age, finding a much wider audience in the process. In many ways, it's a culture still coming to terms with itself and finding its way, with the best still ahead.

Ireland: There are those who feel that Irish music *is* Celtic music. It's certainly the most familiar of the Celtic traditions and the most widely played. In part that's because Ireland lasted so long as a rural economy, where the old ways didn't die. Throughout the countryside, fiddlers played for dances, and the Gaelic songs were passed down in families. But initially there was never a sense of it being a nation's music, as such. Irish musicians were often recorded, for example, the great fiddler Michael Coleman, but these people were only exploring their local traditions. However, those early recordings, such as Coleman's, tended to set the style in stone, and those who came after took from it, creating an "Irish" style.

The first to see the full possibilities of an Irish music was Seán Ó'Riada, a composer and arranger living in the Gaeltacht, or Gaelic-speaking part of Ireland. In the late 1950s, he put together an ensemble to play Irish traditional music (much as groups like the Dubliners and the Clancy Brothers played Irish songs). Some of the musicians he picked went on to form the Chieftains, whose forty-year history and wonderful skills have made them Ireland's most renowned band, and the most famous of all Celtic ensembles. Their early records had a gorgeous purity that first made many people aware of the lilt in Irish music.

The 1970s brought another quantum leap, as groups like Planxty and the Bothy Band brought the energy of rock to traditional music (and also made the Greek bouzouki a staple of the Irish sound). The rock influence brought the traditional Greek music to the attention of the younger generation, which was exactly the injection the music needed to take it to the next level. And rock bands like Horslips (and even Thin Lizzy with their version of the old "Whiskey in the Jar") took an interest.

Throughout the 1980s and 1990s, new artists appeared on the galvanized folk scene, such as accordion and fiddle player Sharon Shannon, Altan, fiddler Martin Hayes, and even the

Pogues, who added the fire of punk—and some fine songs from the pen of Shane MacGowan. The proliferation of talent has been tremendous, and it's helped Irish music expand in many directions, from the folk/pop of the Waterboys to the New Age inflections of Clannad and Enya. The cherry on the sundae, of course, has been the phenomenon called River-dance, which brought together traditionally styled music with step-dancing for an Irish spectacle that's traveled around the world and helped make Irish music the most recognized and embraced Celtic style.

In addition to so many fine instrumentalists, the Emerald Island has also produced plenty of outstanding singers. Sean nós (in the old style) singing in Gaelic is the oldest and has found several modern disciples, such as Iarla O'Liónaird from Afro Celt Sound System and even Sinead O'Connor; but it's the folk songs that have attracted many of the best, like Dolores Keane and Niamh Parsons, who've brought a grace to some very delicate music and spread the old ballads.

England: England's folk music tradition is a long one, one of the oldest elements being the Morris Dance, which has its roots in the Middle Ages. Morris "sides" (as they're known) still exist and perform, and many of the old tunes, such as "Speed the Plough" still survive. Morris dancing, like the maypole tradition, is very rural; and the face of folk music changed with industrialization and the move of much of the populace to the cities. While the old songs remained (and, like Morris dancing, most folk music has stayed intact in rural areas), new styles emerged in the cities. The ballads were printed and distributed on broadsides and often focused on topical matters.

Folk music lost ground in urban areas with the rise of music hall and popular music. The revival of the 1950s, led by

Ewan MacColl, brought a greater awareness, with singers like Shirley Collins and Anne Briggs performing traditional music.

The late 1960s brought electric folk/rock, in the form of Fairport Convention and Steeleye Span, who instigated a revolution. Marrying rock instruments and old folk songs was unheard of, but these groups not only managed it but also sold it to a young generation that didn't care about folk. It was a surface investigation of the tradition, at best (although a few albums, like *No Roses* and *Morris On*, did delve a bit deeper), but it pointed a way forward for a relatively moribund folk scene. By the 1980s, in the wake of punk, roots music had become more underground, with bands like Home Service and the Oyster Band, and singers like the velvet-voiced June Tabor. But the 1990s saw it rise again, with an urgent new generation of voices demanding to be heard.

Traditional English folk music has outgrown its shaggy 1960s image of Aran sweaters and beards to become a musical force once again. While much of the credit must go to guitarist and singer Martin Carthy, M.B.E. (along with his wife, Norma Waterson), much of the inspiration really lies with the Copper Family, who still perform a cappella. The songs they sing have been handed down in their family for more than two hundred years; it's a rare (and dubious) folk performer who doesn't know several Copper Family songs.

Eliza Carthy, the daughter of Carthy and Waterson, has made a string of excellent albums that add her ideas to the English folk lexicon. But she's just one of a growing number, including Kate Rusby and Kathryn Tickell, who have made English folk music exciting once again, full of energy and passion. With so many vibrant performers, the immediate future of the scene looks very healthy.

There's a lot more to music in England than folk, however. The steady flow of immigration since World War II, primarily from Asia and the West Indies, has changed the entire face of the country. Established musical styles have formed new off-shoots and hybrids that have proved quite interesting.

British reggae began in the 1970s, as the children of the first West Indian immigrants were coming of age. Bands like Aswad, Misty in Roots, and Steel Pulse found success; the last on an international level. The lyrical concerns they voiced differed from Jamaican reggae bands, often focusing on racism and other issues of color in a predominantly white society. Perhaps the most articulate spokesman was Linton Kwesi Johnson, a poet who voiced his work over music in a style called dub poetry. While he records less frequently these days, there's still a resonance of truth about all his work.

For Asian youth, the bhangra scene that evolved in the 1980s offered salvation. It was the music of their culture but played in a modern style that was of the time and sounded hip. And bhangra dances were held in places where Asians could gather safely, with little fear of racist problems—an important factor. And the Asian Underground scene, an important component of 1990s British electronica, grew from these beginnings.

And, of course, there are also artists who simply refuse to fall into any category. Perhaps the best example is 3 Mustaphas 3, a wild band of world music enthusiasts who played in many different styles, from Balkan to Latin, with a strong dose of humor added. For example, they adopted names and a background from a fictional Balkan country. Now sadly defunct, their command of so many different styles was astounding, making their albums absolute delights. London-based Afro Celt Sound System is one of a number of bands building from the idea of "ethno-techno" (adding ethnic music to dance beats) with their Celtic-African fusion; others, such as Transglobal Underground, pull sounds from the Middle East and India.

Some artists have tried to address what it means to be English today in multicultural Britain, and it seems there are no easy answers; it's a definition in progress, and it might be another generation before there's a real consensus. The one who perhaps came closest was former Clash member Joe Strummer on his *Global a Go-Go* record, released not long before his untimely death. With conscious effort, he was able to draw together elements of reggae and Indian music behind his edgy rock 'n' roll for a satisfying experience that remained ineffably English.

England is trying to find its place in the twenty-first century. Once a great power, its days of glory are now long gone. But alongside the mix of cultures in England of today, there's also a venerable history that can't simply be ignored. However, no one's managed to completely reconcile those two strands yet. Until someone does, it leaves England with a glowing, multifaceted—but ultimately fragmented—roots music scene.

France: France is the country of existentialism, sidewalk cafés, the chanson and Edith Piaf, and the louche lyrics of Serge Gainsbourg. At least, that's the France of popular imagination. And to an extent it is all those things, but the reality is so much more—North African immigrants have brought their own sound to the cities, and the regions have their own music.

The deepest strain of French folk music lies in Brittany, known to locals as Breizh, the Celtic region of France, off to the West, where the heritage and pride still run strong. Both instrumental and vocal traditions date back several centuries. However, one of the oldest, the Breton harp, had been neglected for many years before Alan Stivell and his father began giving it attention. In the 1970s, Stivell was the shining figure of Breton music, playing a very stirring kind of folk/rock that used many Breton instruments, such as the bagpipes. Although he was the trailblazer, others followed, with Dan Ar Bras and Gabriel Yacoub, both graduates from Stivell's band, becoming important figures in Breton music.

Paris is understandably famous for its café music, with the rich sound of the accordion. The style is actually called bal-musette, and it's been an important part of French music for over a century. While associated with the emotive chanson vocalizing of the great Piaf, it fell by the wayside for a couple of decades and has only recently begun to experience a revival through bands like Paris Combo, who've quickly gained fans with their attractive style.

The other sound of the capital city is unmistakably North African, like the Orchestra National de Barbès, a group of North Africans from different countries, all living in the Barbès quarter of Paris. They make a new sound, a kind of pan-Maghreb music that's influenced by things they've heard in Europe. They're just the beginning of North Africans who are learning to explore the melodic and rhythmic possibilities of a multicultural society.

It's that idea of fusion that's been the fuel of modern French music. The band Mano Negra, which existed from the mid-1980s until 1993, kick-started the movement. Although they were strongly inspired by punk, especially the Clash, they brought in elements from Latin, Arabic, and Balkan music to their hard-edged sound. Singing in a mix of Spanish, French, and English, they replicated the multiculti swirl of the country around them.

The band's leader, Manu Chao, has enjoyed greater success since the band split up. His first solo album did well, but the second, *Proxima Estacion: Esperanza*, made him a world music star, with its bubbly, low-fi soup of reggae, rock, and

Latin music. An iconoclastic figure, Chao is equally comfortable recording on a portable four-track machine in the wilds of South America, working in a state-of-the-art studio, playing on the street in Barcelona (his adopted home), and performing in a stadium.

The idea of cultural fusion is also at the heart of the band Lo'Jo. Although they've existed for twenty years, it's only since 1998 that they've made a mark on the international music scene—but at that point they'd got their mix of sounds just right. Alongside the gruff singing and poetry of leader Denis Péan stood some wild gypsy violin. Two Algerian sisters added the sound of North Africa in their vocals. The rhythm section, meanwhile, could work well with reggae and West African rhythms. It makes for a fascinating stew and one of the best signposts to the future for France, and the band has been refining and experimenting with it ever since, to greater and greater acclaim.

It's really only within the past half decade that French music seems to have found its voice, or rather its many voices. From the smooth rap of MC Solaar to dub and to the strong Mediterranean inflections of Marseille's Massillia Sound System, France has become louder and more important.

Spain: Think Spain, and the chances are you'll think flamenco, with its guitar flourishes, clicking castanets, and smoldering dancers. It's true, flamenco is the music most associated with Spain. It's a demanding art for singers, instrumentalists, and dancers, trying to reach that moment of duende, or transcendence.

Flamenco originated in the Rajahstan area of India, traveling west with the Romany people. Along the way it was colored by the sounds and rhythms of the Middle East and the Mediterranean. While there's still a strong Romany element in the music, you'll find plenty of non-Gypsies playing the music these days.

The Gypsy Kings have become flamenco's global brand name, and they've certainly had a huge commercial impact with their appealing mix of flamenco and rumba. To dig down to the music's roots, however, with its classic repertoire, listen to singer El Camarón de la Isla, whose weary voice was born for flamenco.

The guitar works with the singer to create the song, and one of the very best guitarists is Paco de Lucia, whose mastery of the fretboard is second to none. He also helped expand the genre, bringing in some Brazilian influences, which opened the door for Nueva Flamenco, a style that's added rock, Latin, and North African music (among others). Done right, as with Ketama, it can be stunning; however, that's a rarity.

Flamenco is centered in Andalucía, the region where it's grown and developed. Go to another part of Spain, and you'll hear something completely different. In the northern Basque area they play trikitrixa, a traditional bagpipe style that's usually played on accordion. One of the best, and certainly most adventurous, players in the style is Kepa Junkera. With an impeccable technique and an abundant imagination, he's drawing trikitrixa out of its homeland and onto the global stage; his *Bilbao 00:00h* was a tour de force that melded his accordion work with many other European forms.

Fermin Muguruza is also from the Basque country, but his music couldn't be more different. Influenced by punk, hip-hop, and ska, he's confrontational, political, demanding, and decidedly modern.

The biggest revelation in Spanish music, though, has been the blossoming of the sounds from Galicia, after many dormant years. Galicia is one of Europe's Celtic regions on the edge of the Atlantic, and it shares many musical traits with

Ireland, Scotland, and Brittany. Like virtually all Spanish regional music, it received no encouragement during all the years Franco was in power, although there was enough local support to ensure it never died. Within the past ten years it's truly taken off and found its place within both Celtic and world music.

It's Galician pipers who've made the most impact, notably Carlos Nuñez, who's done a great deal to resurrect the proud Galician piping tradition. A virtuoso, he was a member of Ireland's Chieftains for a short time, exploring the connections between his native music and theirs. More recently, he's explored links between the music of Galicia and several other cultures, including North Africa. While Nuñez's approach can sometimes be a little academic, another piper, Susana Seivane, is simply carrying on the family tradition. She might not display the lightning-fast fingers of Nuñez, but her style is more rooted in music passed down through generations.

Portugal: If flamenco is the passionate heart of Spain, then the music known as fado is the soul of Portugal. The term, which translates literally as "fate," is perhaps an apt description for a music that's choked with yearning (or *saudade*, the closest Portuguese equivalent). It's about the stuff of life—the broken hearts, the poverty, the constant battles of daily living— and accepting it. In that regard, fado resembles the blues (to which it's sometimes compared), or Cape Verdean morna, as the music of the downtrodden.

Also like blues, its origins are uncertain, although it can be traced back to the working-class district of nineteenth-century Lisbon, where it was performed by female singers in the small bars that lined the streets (and where it's still possible to find fado bars today).

While the music's developed a little over the years, its

essence has remained simple: a voice singing poetry over an accompaniment of viola (not the viola of classical music, but the name given locally to the Spanish guitar) and the guitarra, often referred to as the Portuguese guitar, with its six pairs of strings tuned a specific way. It makes for a unique, immediately identifiable, and dramatic sound behind the emotive singer.

And of those singers, the queen was Amália Rodrigues. She made fado into the form it is today, bringing it out of the back streets and into the concert halls of the world. Her voice, able to capture tiny nuances of emotion, could—and did—enchant. She expanded the genre, singing in Spanish and using an orchestra instead of a small group, while never losing the aching quality of fado.

It's the fadistas, the female vocalists, who've largely carried fado. Although there have been a few male singers of note, among the new generation helping the music blossom again, the voices are all those of women. Cristina Branco, with a wonderfully pure voice and delicate delivery, has already proved herself to be a leading light of "traditional" fado, though her lyrics come from modern poets. Misia is more experimental, adding piano and other instruments not generally considered part of the style. Newcomer Mariza seems to walk a line between the others, with respect for the tradition but her eyes set on the future.

Fado is Lisbon's music, but Lisbon isn't Portugal any more than New York is the United States. Outside the capital there's a thriving roots music scene. Dulce Pontes, for example, has managed a long and successful singing career that's carried her from pop to folk, and even fado, performing with credibility while being a big star. More political, and concerned with social issues, is Brigada Victor Jara. Now more than a quarter of a century old (and containing no original members), the band continues to explore Portugal's folk traditions, while several former members have gone on to make their mark on national music.

Italy: The range of music within Italy is quite staggering. Each region, it seems, has a developed tradition, to the point where cataloging them all would be almost impossible. But certain areas do have commonalties. Throughout much of southern Italy, for example, they've long danced the tarantella, an ancient, wild possession dance, supposedly derived from a sacred dance to heal a deadly spider's bite. With lively, syncopated movements, it forms the basis of much of the music in the Neopolitan region.

Politically, the area is strongly left leaning, and groups like E'Zezi (formed from workers at the Alfa Romeo plant) have combined politics with roots music for a potent mixture. A recent offshoot of that group, Spaccanapoli, even sings in the local dialect, mixing voices with acoustic and electric instruments to the beat of the tamura, or frame drum (these portable, hand-held drums—made from a skin stretched over a frame—occur in many different cultures, with different names, such as the Irish bodhran).

One of the more fascinating traditions isn't from Italy itself but from the islands of Sardinia and Corsica. The polyphonic singing of the male tenors (*tenores*) is weirdly wonderful, with three-part harmonies that initially seem unlikely but that resolve themselves perfectly, creating the illusion of a fourth part. There's been a renewed interest in the style, following the international success of I. Muvrini and Tenores de Bitti, who have become emblematic of the singular island style. Others, like Tenores de Oniferi, have also released records.

In Sicily you can hear the old songs of honor that are at the heart of the Mafia, or listen to the radical brass band style of

Banda Ionica, who rework old sacred music in a highly individual manner.

Curiously, the music of central and northern Italy has never received as much exposure. It's certainly not for a lack of variety, with artists like singer Giovanna Marini, who's done much to push the cause of roots music in Italy, or Riccardo Tesso, one of the leading exponents of the Italian accordion music called organetti.

Greece: The music of Greece is much more than that heard in *Zorba the Greek* or the film music of Mikis Theodorakis, wonderful as that is. But two types of music unite the country.

What fado is to Portugal, or raï to Algeria, rembetika is to Greece. It's the music of the underclasses, the disenfranchised, and the people who exist on the fringes of society. While there are speculations about its origins—some believe it arrived with the Greeks of Turkey, who were forcibly repatriated after World War I—no one seems to be certain where it really began. But by the 1920s it became popular in the poorest quarters of the major Greek cities, the voices accompanied by the long-necked lute called the bouzouki.

The music was pushed down and repressed during the 1967–1974 junta. After that, it returned full force, as many musicians explored the old songs. One of the first was Yiorgos (George) Dalaras, who'd already won national fame as a singer/songwriter, and whose career continues to flourish. Among the most notable is Eleftheria Arvanitaki. She began in rembetika and still sings and records it. These days, however, she has songs composed for her (in Greece, as in the Middle East, the singer/songwriter is a rarity; composers and lyricists write the songs, and the singer performs them).

Rembetika is soulful music, but it's not Greece's favorite.

That title belongs to laïkó, or Greek popular music. It came to the fore in the 1950s, and Haris Alexiou, one of the early stars, has retained her fan base through the decades. As with most pop music, it went out of fashion, to return in the 1980s with a harder edge. It is interesting that Alexiou, with her remarkably expressive voice, has adapted her style and stayed a star in the new laïkó.

The Greek islands have long enjoyed their own music, and in Crete the lyre (or lyra), an instrument that can be seen on classical Greek friezes, still plays an active part in the local music, connecting the past very much to the present.

Hungary: While Gypsy music is important in Hungary, there's also a strong indigenous folk scene that's existed for several centuries. Classical composers Béla Bartók and Zoltán Kodály both collected folk music in the early 1900s, covering not only Hungary itself but also Transylvania. Although the traditions dwindled in a world that changed after two world wars, they do still persist in rural areas.

An album of songs Bartók had collected was released by the band Muzsikás, one of the brand names of Hungarian music. Either alone or working with vocalist Márta Sebestyén, they've created an impressive body of work covering Hungary, the Jewish music of Transylvania, and music pulled from the villages. Sebestyén has become a star in her own right (she was featured on the soundtrack of the movie *The English Patient*). In addition to exploring the Hungarian tradition, she's experimented with beats and loops, and with music from as far away as India and Ireland.

Bulgaria: Bulgarian folk music is mostly dance music, springing off complex rhythms. It's often heard at weddings, which are the big social occasions. The parties can last for days, and the musicians put on plenty of entertainment. Ivo Papasov began on the wedding circuit, but the clarinetist with the dazzling technique has had a mark internationally by fusing traditional music with jazz.

For many people in the United States, their first real taste of world music came at the end of the 1980s with the Bulgarian Women's Choir on an album called *Le Mystère des Voix Bulgares*. They're actually the National Radio and Television Chorus (and, in fact, do work full time for radio and television), and their repertoire does really come from Bulgarian villages, brought by the choir members themselves. Mixing harmony and startling dissonance, they use a lot of diaphonic (two-part) singing, in which single voices or whole choral sections shift at unusual musical intervals. To outside ears it can sound chillingly eerie. They use a specific vocal technique that's been preserved in Bulgaria, with a small vocal range of around an octave that creates a powerful, piercing sound. The choir's French name, by the way, came from the original compilation of music that Marcel Cellier, a Swiss musicologist, pieced together from the archives of Bulgarian Television and Radio.

They're one of several ensembles in the country, such as the more compact Trio Bulgarka (who even added their special harmonies to a Kate Bush album), or the seminal, thirty-four-member Philip Koutev National Folk Ensemble.

Germany: It's perhaps strange that Germany, one of Europe's most developed countries, has made next to no impact on the world music scene. But the folk music scene has never completely recovered from World War II; folk music exists, but the country's focus has been largely on modernism. With a large immigrant population, many from the Balkan areas, the country is still in a state of musical flux.

Gypsy Music

The music of the Gypsy, or Romany, people can be heard across Europe. It's in the traveling people of Britain and in Spain's flamenco. But it's most evident in the Balkans.

One of the historical roles of the Romany people has been as musicians (indeed, the image of the Gypsy violinist has become a romantic stereotype). In part, that's been because it was one of the few jobs available in societies that were habitually prejudiced against the Romany. So they made their living traveling around, playing for weddings, circumcisions, and dances. They needed to be familiar with many different styles and often imparted new ideas to local musicians, while also learning from them; they were adaptable to almost any situation. During the nineteenth century, for example, much of the Ashkenazi Jewish music from Eastern Europe, called klezmer, was actually played by Gypsies.

In Macedonia, you frequently find Gypsy brass bands, and village bands occur throughout the Balkans, an indicator of just how entwined Gypsy and Balkan music can be. Usually playing at incredible speed, their technical ability is staggering. While the stars are outfits like Fanfare Ciocărlia, Boban Markovic, and the Kocani Orkestar, a visit to the annual Dragacevo Brass festival quickly proves that high standards are the norm, not the exception.

It's the violin that people associate with Gypsies, however, and there's no shortage of that. From Sandor Fodor to the remarkable Taraf de Haïdouks, the violin music can be quietly beautiful or wildly pulse pounding. The Romanian Taraf de Haïdouks have become the standard for Gypsy violin bands. From Clejani, they're a true village band with fiddles and cimbalon (a kind of hammer dulcimer) and execute some of the most skillful playing to be found anywhere.

While the roots of much European Gypsy music lie in the Middle East and India, it's largely been diluted over the years. But if you listen to Gypsy music from Turkey, such as the Istanbul Oriental Ensemble, it's easy to trace the connection. Again, the players are outstanding, and their repertoire, some of which reaches back a few hundred years, covers much of the Gypsy presence.

There are also bands across the Balkans looking to the future. They haven't turned their backs on their heritage; instead they're trying to expand it and claim a place in tomorrow. Besh o Drom, for instance, employ traditional instruments but also use sampling and a DJ as part of their arsenal, integrating the techniques well to excellent effect. As with all folk traditions, constant reinvention keeps the music fresh.

The instrumentalists are the entertainers, and their dexterity and virtuosity can be staggering. But there are also some excellent Romany vocalists. Macedonian Esma Redzepova has emerged from her own country to claim an international following with her big, emotive voice. But it's Vera Bilá who's been anointed as the queen. Born in Slovakia, she now lives in the Czech Republic. Adding soft Brazilian rhythms to Gypsy song, she's created a curious, attractive blend of the raw and the sophisticated as a backdrop for her intoxicating voice. Now she tours the world, although at home she and her band, Kale (Vera Bilá and Kale translates as Vera White and the Blacks), still suffer prejudice because they're Gypsies.

Dissidenten is probably Germany's leading world music band. Together for more than twenty years, the group's explorations have extended beyond North Africa, taking in India, Hawaii, and native North American music, absorbing it and being involved with it, rather than simply appropriating it. They've been among the pioneers of world music, albeit often unsung simply because they did start so early. They're still active, regularly producing challenging but accessible new records.

The Americas

From the tip of Tierra del Fuego to the icy wastes far north of the Arctic Circle, the New World of the Americas is truly a musical melting pot; everyone has come from elsewhere. Even the indigenous people of the continent arrived over the land bridge that once existed as a link to Siberia. White colonization by the Spanish, French, Portuguese, and English wrought huge changes. The importation of slaves from Africa—only a small portion of whom ended up in the United States—altered everything again. Waves of immigration through the late nineteenth and early twentieth centuries again changed the face of the Americas.

That's not to say other ethnic groups haven't had an effect. European immigrants brought the roots of the tango and klezmer. The German polkas, played by immigrants in south Texas, form the basis for norteño, or Tex-Mex music. Perhaps the greatest thing about the Americas is the way things have been adapted and altered to fit new circumstances; just like the people, music is an immigrant, finding its way in a new land.

The African influence is most evident in the Caribbean and down the east coast of South America (although it extends much farther). Their rhythms have made samba, reggae, and Cuban son, even though the styles sound very different, just as they've made blues and jazz. And no country in the New World became the home of more slaves than Brazil.

Brazil: *Samba* and *bossa nova* are terms most people have heard, even if they couldn't recognize the music. They're two of the styles that help make Brazil such a rich musical country and one of the most diverse.

But samba remains the music most associated with Brazil. The rhythmic and melodic sophistication belie its roots in the *favelas*, or shanty towns, of Río, in the early part of the twentieth century. It was the heavily syncopated music the poor made for the annual carnaval—loud, very African, and offensive to the white upper classes with their sedate European choro parlor music (and, ironically, samba was the melodies of choro and other European dance musics, filtered through African syncopation).

Samba stuck around, becoming more popular and developing several strands. The samba de enredo is the sound of the massive samba schools, with their elaborate costumes and routines, in competition with each other at carnaval. More familiar perhaps, is samba de canção, or samba song. But even that has become a generic term for several different subgenres.

For much of the first half of the twentieth century, samba ruled the roost. Competition arrived in the 1950s from bossa nova (literally, "new beat"), the cooler, more sophisticated sound of the Río beaches that mixed samba and jazz. The creation of guitarist Antonio Carlos Jobim, it was first voiced by singer and guitarist João Gilberto (whose daughter, Bebel, is a well respected singer today). Soft and sultry, it was instantly successful. By the end of the decade it had hit the United States, where Astrud Gilberto's "The Girl from Ipanema" introduced the new sound. It was quickly picked up by jazz players who sensed the airiness of the melodies and who continued to mine the music throughout the 1960s. Bossa nova remains an important part of Brazilian music, but it was eclipsed in the 1960s by MPB, or Brazilian popular music, which took the strands of what had gone before.

Just as the United States and Britain underwent enormous social and music changes in the mid-1960s, so did Brazil. The movement called tropicália challenged everything extant in Brazilian music. While still ineffably Brazilian, it brought in elements of rock, with loud electric instruments, willfully arty, obscure lyrics, and even performance art. Led by singer/songwriters Caetano Veloso and Gilberto Gil, the movement's challenge to the establishment—both musical and political—didn't go unnoticed; the pair was forced into exile in England for a few years. On their return they found themselves icons of the new MPB scene, where they've remained ever since. In fact, Gil is now Brazil's minister of culture, and Veloso is acknowledged as the country's leading musical figure.

They both came from Bahia, in the north of Brazil, where African rhythms play much closer to the surface and the old religion of *candomblé* is easy to find. It's been one of the country's most fertile musical areas, the home of singers Maria Bethânia (Veloso's half-sister), Gal Costa, Margareth Menezes, and Daniela Mercury, among many others. Mercury was one of the biggest names of the 1990s, with her percussive axé sound. Energetic, and very crisply rhythmic, it walks the fine line between roots and pop well. She's recorded with Olodum, the drum-based band who helped out Paul Simon (on *Rhythm of the Saints*) while also becoming Brazilian stars in their own right.

MPB has become the catch-all name for most Brazilian music, from the honeyed singing of Milton Nascimento, one of the most talented singer/songwriters to emerge from Brazil, to the electronica of Naçao Zumbi. It's wide-ranging, but that's the point. Unlike the pop music of much of the Western Hemisphere, however, it's strongly rooted in tradition, and the stars don't vanish overnight, although new ones appear regularly. Both Chico Cesar and Marisa Monte had emerged at the head of the pack by the end of the 1990s.

If the music of any country could be said to be going "forward in all directions," it's Brazil. From the lambada, which was originally dance music from Bahia before it was co-opted and diluted into a brief international pop craze, to the forró of the very northeast—a kind of Brazilian Cajun music—there are no limits, it seems.

One of the unifying factors of Brazilian music is its sophistication. While that can sometimes mean it's mistaken for easy listening music, don't be fooled. There's always a strong, deep intelligence going on, no matter what the style. That's immediately apparent in the rhythms. Whether stated or implied, the polyrhythms create a bed for the music, adding immeasurably to the music. Indeed, Brazilian percussionists like Aitro Moreira and Carlinhos Brown (who's also a major songwriter) are world renowned and in demand.

Argentina: Argentina's great contribution to world music has been the tango, the forbidden dance of Buenos Aires. It's eclipsed the country's other musical forms, such as chamamé (which, like tango, is accordion or bandoneon based). And tango did indeed have its origins in the city's bordellos and bars at the start of the twentieth century; it was quickly exported to France and other European countries.

But few people have really heard authentic Argentinian tango, only the less potent foreign versions. Originally it was danced in brothels, the musical style imported from Africa via the West Indies, and combined with the music of the Spanish colonists. The nuevo tango of bandoneon player Astor Piazzolla, however, has fans around the world. Classically trained, he began experimenting with tango in 1960, never losing its sensual aspect but turning it into art music, to be heard rather than danced to. By the end of his career, he'd succeeded in making tango a classical form.

Piazzolla might have been Argentina's greatest artist, but the country's most formidable singer has long been a thorn in the side of the country's government. Mercedes Sosa came to prominence as part of the pan-Latin political nueva canción movement of the 1960s. She was exiled in 1978 for her politics and allowed back home in 1982. But that didn't silence her, and she's remained a very vocal critic of government policies—as well as being a fine singer.

Chile: The Andean music of the native peoples is Chile's great tradition, one it shares with Peru and Argentina. But the country is more associated with the nueva canción of the 1960s, which modernized the traditional folk music and proved popular all across South America, and was the soundtrack to the spirit of revolution that was in the air. It gave a voice to Chile's great singer/songwriter Victor Jara. He wrote about the people, about their real lives, rather than anything idealized or romanticized. A supporter of Allende, he was tortured and casually murdered by General Pinochet's soldiers in 1973; his fate was discovered only because he was recognized by a mortuary worker.

His life was cut tragically short, but his music has lived on, recorded by many English and American rock stars. He was a direct influence on Inti-Illimani, whose politics took the form of solidarity with the Andean people, playing their instruments and adopting their clothing. They were in Europe in 1973 as ambassadors for Allende's government when the September 11 coup happened, and the Continent became their home for the next fifteen years. They toured regularly, becoming a fixture in several countries. In the end, they arrived back in Chile on the day Pinochet's government was voted out by the people. Still recording and touring, they've stayed true to the Andean music that inspired them.

Those days of terror have passed in Chile. A new generation of bands have appeared, for whom politics is just one facet of their music. Gondwana, for instance, use reggae as their means of expression (showing that the style has no geographic limitations).

Peru: Like Chile, Peru is associated with the lyrical Andean music of the natives, with the ringing, trebly sound of the charango and the lull of the panpipes. It's not all Peruvian—the Andes run through Chile and Argentina as well—but the peasant image of the musicians certainly is. There are plenty of such bands with varying degrees of talent, but they form only one part of the area's traditional music. The traditional music of Peru extends from the more familiar sounds of the mountain areas to the relatively unknown coastal regions.

Something often forgotten is that African slaves were also transported to Peru, and that a sizable Afro-Peruvian population exists within the country. For many years their music and culture were overlooked. It's largely been just within the past four decades that the highly rhythmic sound has broken out of its ghetto, and within the past twenty years that it's been seen as credible. While diva Susana Baca is the big name, with several lauded albums to her credit, she's far from being the only act making waves: Pepe Vasquez has become a star at home by marrying traditional Peruvian festejo (festive music) with Afro-Peruvian rhythms.

Colombia: Colombia's great claim to fame is cumbia, the national dance rhythm, syncopated and multilayered with wonderfully light melodies. It's still performed by traditional cumbia ensembles around the country. It's also become a major pan-Latin rhythm, particularly popular in Mexico.

Toto La Momposina is the queen of Colombian roots music, performing cumbia, along with the music of her native island of Mompos on the northern Colombian coast. Mixing the sound of the Indians, runaway black slaves, and the influence of the Spanish colonizers, she's become an attraction on the world music festival circuit with her presentation of traditional music, song, and dance. It's a show, but one that's true to the history of the people and the music.

Colombia's been one of the most successful exporters of modern Latin music. Probably most people who've listened to Latin pop know it's the home of Shakira. She's the commercial superstar, but her music doesn't have that much to do with her native land. Far more rooted, while still rocking, is Los Aterciopelados, a two-piece band from Bogota, who made their name as one of the most creative Rock en Español groups during the 1990s before experimenting with electronica. However, the rhythms under their music come from bolero, mariachi, and especially cumbia. They've achieved a reasonable amount of commercial success abroad, even winning a Grammy. Singer Carlos Vives is another of the country's biggest names, a star of TV soap operas who turned very convincingly to music, transforming the coastal vallenato rhythm into something urban and modern, while still managing to retain its traditional flavor—and a lot of its traditional instrumentation.

Trinidad and Tobago: Trinidad has given the world one of the simplest, but at the same time most complex, music forms— calypso. Its popular image is of a man with a guitar singing humorous or satirical songs. And it can indeed be that, but calypso is also a fully orchestrated art form, and every year at carnival the top artists battle it out for the crown.

Its origins lie in African music, with layers of Spanish and English colonialism on top (the word *calypso* was actually first applied to a dance, not a song). At the end of the nineteenth century, at the annual carnival, the "chantwells," as they were called, would sing, composing topical songs. The tradition of calypso tents at carnival began in the 1920s, when the chantwells would perform, backed by touring vaudeville bands from Guyana.

The golden age of calypso began properly in the 1930s, with performers like Roaring Lion (one of the genre's great innovators), Atilla the Hun, Lord Invader, and others—all of whom enjoyed careers lasting several decades. Lord Invader even had a U.S. hit, when the Andrews Sisters covered his song "Rum and Coca Cola," although he had to sue to ever see royalties. And calypso even became a brief fad in the United States during the 1950s, thanks to Harry Belafonte's *Calypso* album, while West Indian immigrants brought it to England.

Famous for political and social commentary, the calypsonians could be cutting—and also quick witted, as one of the style's traits has always been extemporization.

By the 1970s, calypso was in decline and found itself replaced by the more uptempo soca (a word made from joining soul and calypso), kick-started by Lord Shorty. But it went worldwide thanks to the success of Arrow's "Hot Hot Hot," although recent years have seen the style supplanted by rapso—a mix of rap and soca.

Calypso still rules the carnival, however, covering several tents each year; and every one is crowded with stars and aspiring calypsonians. The great old masters might have passed on (many of them living to surprising ages), but artists like Black Stalin, Calypso Rose, and David Rudder have kept the flame burning bright.

There's also a lesser-known Trinidadian subgenre affectionately called chutney (a reference to the Indian condiment). More than a hundred years ago, after the slaves had been emancipated, the British recruited laborers from India to work the West Indian sugar plantations. Many stayed, and their descendents remain, with their own customs—and music, which merged with soca and other Caribbean music to create a new, energetic hybrid.

Guadeloupe, Martinique: The islands that make up the French Antilles—especially Guadeloupe and Martinique—gave the world some of the most danceable music of the late 1970s and early 1980s. Zouk, as it was known, mixed up West African soukous, with its rippling guitars, the bouncing rhythms of Caribbean pop, Creole singing, and the irresistible bass of American funk.

But the music is rooted in the Antillean gwo ka tradition. It is centered around the drums but includes dance and singing, and is still performed today. With the other layers added, it became zouk.

The French connection of the islands meant the music was played in the Paris discos, then the most cosmopolitan and trend-setting in Europe. It was possibly the first world music to have a broad impact, even if it wasn't felt in the United States, giving it a special significance that shouldn't be underestimated. It made stars of bands like Kassav', who'd been at the forefront of the new music. And they stayed there, constantly bringing new elements into their sound throughout the 1980s and 1990s to assert their dominance. Individual members, particularly singer Jocelyne Beroard, have also juggled successful careers. Zouk might have slipped out of European trendiness a few years ago, but it remains tremendously popular in the Antilles, and Kassav' have never gone out of style.

Nor have Malavoi, although they take a completely different approach to music. Classically trained, the group takes the colonial dances of former times, such as the mazurka and the waltz, then adds touches of rumba and other Caribbean and

Latin styles. Their heyday seemed to end at the beginning of the 1990s, although recent releases have begun to hint at a renaissance.

Bahamas: Not a great deal of Africa remains in the former British colony of the Bahamas. The links across the Atlantic largely died during the twentieth century. What remains is celebrated in the annual junkanoo festival at New Year, using the thundering goombay drum, whose ancestors are definitely West African. The Baha Men took the traditional sounds of junkanoo and the goombay drum, mixed them with pop and hip-hop, and scored global hits with infectious songs like "Who Let the Dogs Out?"

At the other end of the spectrum is Joseph Spence, one of the world's most individual guitarists. He made his home here, and his influence on more than one generation of guitar players in England and the United States is quite profound.

Haiti: Think of Haiti, and you imagine one of the poorest countries in the world, whose politics were shattered by years of violent totalitarianism under the Duvaliers. It's also the Caribbean home of voodoo, which brings together the beliefs of the African slaves who were brought here with the Catholicism imparted by their colonial masters. In vodou, drumming and chants play a vital role in the ceremonies—the primal traditional black music of Haiti. The white population that ruled the island brought European music—the quadrilles, minuetes, and other dances.

Far more than vodou, it was the European sounds that influenced the Haitian beat called compas. Compas mixes together several Caribbean and European styles and can easily be heard in the music of Tabou Combo, and even in the hip-hop of the Fugees, whose leader, Wyclef Jean, comes from Haiti.

However, if it's real roots you're looking for, go back to the early albums by Boukman Eksperyans. With voodoo chants, powerful percussion, and electric instruments touching on reggae and funk, they're redolent of the real Haiti, and they have been threatened by the authorities several times during their career. Recent records, however, have seemed bland and diluted, as if the fire that possessed them before had died.

Dominican Republic: The Dominican Republic shares the island of Hispaniola with Haiti, but there are radical differences in both the politics and the music of the two countries. Wherever you go in the Dominican Republic, you'll hear merengue, which has become the nation's signature rhythm and one of the main pan-Latin dance beats. It's developed from its acoustic roots, with heavily Africanized polyrhythms elaborating a 4/4 beat, into powerful pop. The main name in Dominican merengue, without doubt, has to be Juan Luis Guerra. He's been an innovator since 1984, broadening the scope of the music by bringing in Western pop harmonies, a touch of the rural Dominican bolero-type bachata, and smoothing off all the edges. It's made him into a superstar throughout the Latin world, with music that's far from simplistic and has plenty of lyrical depth, well beyond the range of most pop.

Merengue has proved to be one of the most adaptable rhythms, which means it's cropped up in many areas. You can find it in some Latin hip-hop, and it was often found underpinning house music during the early 1990s.

Jamaica: Jamaica, reggae, and Bob Marley are so intertwined in the minds of most people that they might as well be one thing. But while Marley remains *the* international icon of roots reggae, he's far from being all of it; indeed, reggae is only one part—albeit a very major one—of Jamaica's musical history.

The Jamaican economy, like that of much of the Americas, was built on the back of slavery. Jamaica, though, was one of the few places to have a successful slave rebellion, leaving a legacy of black strength that would run through the teachings of Marcus Garvey and his "return to Africa" campaign in the early part of the twentieth century and characterize the dreadlocked Rastafarians, who survived many years of prejudice and harassment to become one of the island's most powerful cultural forces. Rasta nyabinghi drumming has been an important part of the Jamaican musical scene since the early 1960s—even the Rolling Stones have featured it.

The real story of Jamaican music, though, starts with the mento folk style of the 1940s and 1950s. With some passing similarities to calypso, it was a simple music and is still played by the long-running Jolly Boys. These days, however, it's mostly entertainment at the tourist hotels. It was the first recorded Jamaican music, put on disc in the 1950s by Stanley Motta. However, that wasn't the style that was getting people moving at the sound system dances. The sound systems were, in essence, giant mobile discos, a cheap form of entertainment for the islanders. They'd play the latest R&B releases from the United States, digging to find obscure titles, and competition between the systems was fierce.

That was fine as long as R&B remained a major musical form. But as American tastes changed, and fewer R&B sides were cut, the sound systems needed fresh music. That really spurred the beginnings of the Jamaican recording industry, although for a few years they stuck to recording homegrown R&B music. There was, however, a local twist, with the influence of the New Orleans second-line rhythm evident in the music.

It wasn't until 1960 that Jamaica started to find its musical identity. A number of people have taken credit for ska; but however it really started will probably never be known. The new beat, with its accents shifted to the second and fourth beats of the bar, was a revelation that sparked a revolution. Coming at the same time as Jamaican independence, it became the sound that swept the country, making stars of singers like Jimmy Cliff (whose career is still going strong), Derrick Morgan, and instrumental group the Skatalites. The Skatalites, all skilled musicians with jazz backgrounds, were the house band at the Studio One label.

For several years ska was the sound of Jamaica. In 1963 along came a precocious young talent named Bob Marley, who, as part of the Wailers, was soon scoring Jamaican hits. And in 1964, ska enjoyed its first global smash with Millie's "My Boy Lollipop" (arranged by legendary jazz and ska guitarist Ernest Ranglin).

The winds of change were sweeping through, both in politics and music—and the slower rock-steady rhythm of the mid-1960s reflected the attempt to keep a lid on the escalating political violence. Many of the ska stars remained popular, while the style brought some new names to the fore, like Alton Ellis, John Holt, and Ken Boothe.

Reggae took over from rock steady in 1968 (possibly the first reggae record was "Do the Reggay," by Toots and the Maytals). A fair number of the musicians were Rastafarians, who preached their message in their songs. The new style brought in new performers and producers, people like Lee Perry, whose work behind the control boards was influential on many careers (including that of the Wailers), and young artists like Burning Spear and Gregory Isaacs.

It was 1973 when reggae first really broke out of Jamaica. There had been some hits, principally in Britain, but they were more pop songs than any concerted movement. With the release of the Wailers' *Catch a Fire,* though, all that changed. Remixed for a white rock audience, with a few instruments added, it began the transformation of Bob Marley into a global superstar. His songwriting matured, while the band became simply one of the best in any style of music.

In his wake came plenty of others, and reggae itself expanded to take in toasting (a kind of proto-rap), personified by artists like Big Youth and U-Roy, and dub (sonic experiments in the mixing of a track), typified by the work of King Tubby, Augustus Pablo (who popularized the melodica within reggae), and Keith Hudson.

It was a remarkably fertile time for reggae, or roots reggae as it would come to be known. Many long-established artists, like Toots and the Maytals and Jimmy Cliff, produced their best work, while newcomers such as Black Uhuru brought a wild creative energy. Their rhythm section, of bassist Robbie Shakespeare and drummer Sly Dunbar, developed what was called the rockers sound, a harder take on the old rock-steady rhythm.

Everything changed with the death of Marley in 1981. Black Uhuru stayed popular, but the roots scene seemed to suddenly run out of energy. It was time for something new, and what was appearing was dancehall—singer and DJs on top of rhythm (or riddim) tracks. Often the same rhythm would be voiced by many different artists in their individual ways. The first stars to emerge from dancehall was singer Barrington Levy, followed by DJs (in Jamaica, the toaster or rapper is called a DJ) Yellowman and Eek-A-Mouse.

With dancehall came a new trend. Roots reggae lyrics had been "conscious," or concerned with the spirit and with justice. In the new music, "slackness," or sexual content, some of it quite explicit, became the norm. Then, in 1985, "Under Me

Sleng Teng" appeared, and turned Jamaican music upside down again. It was the first disc not to use live musicians in the studio—everything, including the drums, was done on a Casio keyboard. Suddenly the concept of the studio had been radically revised. Session musicians were barely needed any more—on most discs there might be two human players. It ushered in the style called ragga (short for ragamuffin) with its "gun songs," tales of violence very much akin to gangsta rap, delivered in a high-speed fashion. By the early 1990s violence, slackness, and extreme homophobia were prevalent in the Jamaican charts.

Slowly, the pendulum began to swing the other way. Buju Banton and Beenie Man began bringing in "cultural" (the new word for *conscious*) lyrics, followed by other dancehall icons, like Shabba Ranks and Capleton. Along with singers such as Luciano and Beres Hammond, they've made Rasta ideals relevant again.

Although no longer fashionable in Jamaica, roots reggae has retained its popularity worldwide. Bob Marley remains a hero to many throughout Africa and Latin America, and the artists who performed through the 1970s still find audiences throughout Europe and the United States.

While reggae has always been male dominated (with the exception of a softer late 1970s hybrid called lovers rock), with females assigned the roles of backup or duet vocalists, in recent years women have come more to the fore, as artists like Lady Saw and Lady G. have made a splash in the dancehall. However, their reputation has come as much for the slackness of their lyrics (out-raunching their male counterparts) as for their vocal talent.

In addition to the actual sounds of reggae, it's worth re-membering that Jamaican music has been the source of much that's now taken for granted in modern music. The remix, a staple in dance clubs, originated with Jamaican "version" (a reworking of a tune) and dub. The roots of hip-hop and rap lie in Jamaican toasting. For a small island, it's put out a lot of music.

Cuba: Cuba could easily challenge Jamaica as the most musical island in the Caribbean. Many people first discovered it through *Buena Vista Social Club,* the fabulously successful album and movie that looked back fondly at a lush, golden, pre-Castro era of Cuban *son* (or song).

Unlike Jamaica, though, whose musical rise is relatively recent, Cuban music has some very deep roots, stretching firmly back to Africa. You can hear it in the Yoruba religious music of santeria, whose drumming and songs praise the *orishas* (spirits). And Africa is there in the rumba. Stripped to its essence, rumba is music for voice and percussion, real Afro-Cuban music (indeed, rumba has crossed back and forth between Cuba and West Africa through the years, adding influences and ideas each time).

Rumba is the main African element, but in the more formal danzón you can hear the sound of Europe, filtered through the island sensibility. It's son, however, that fully expresses the heart and soul of the people. Quite where it began, no one really knows, but it's become Cuba's pervasive music, first noted at the beginning of the twentieth century. As the name implies, it's music to be sung; the loose polyrhythms spring around the beat, and the sound of the tres (a Cuban guitar with three pairs of strings, each pair tuned together) lifts it high.

Over the course of a few decades, son developed. Band-leader Arsenio Rodríguez worked it heavily in the 1940s, broadening the possibilities and making it music for a full band, including descarga, or improvisational, sections for the musicians to show their chops.

Rodríguez was influential, but the crown went to band-leader and sonero Beny Moré. Still considered to be the greatest singer of son, he was one of the main figures of the 1950s, a true musical giant, equally at home with all types of Latin music, including the fiery mambo, which became such a fad in the United States that it powered the first craze for Latin music in the 1950s.

It's impossible to separate Cuban music from the country's politics. Before Castro, the country was wide open, drawing plenty of Americans to its casinos and beaches, while orchestras and singers entertained in the many hotels. Once Castro took power in the 1959 revolution, everything changed. Many musicians left to live and work in the United States. Those who remained faced many years of hardship, with few chances for foreign exposure.

There were compensations, however. Socialism meant that promising musicians received conservatory training in Havana, and professional musicians were paid by the state, although their wage was just a pittance. Throughout the 1970s and 1980s, musicians continued to defect.

Cuban music did develop, however. Bands like Los Van Van and NG La Banda (formed by a former Los Van Van member) pushed up the Afro-Cuban quotient, bringing in a number of innovations, while jazz groups like Irakere mixed Cuban music and modern jazz for a highly individual sound. And they were just a few of many groups playing music around the island. Sierra Maestra played son pure and straight, whereas Eliades Ochoa, who led the Cuarteto Patria, played a more rural, string-based sound.

The music was there, but very little of it was being released outside Cuba. And that wouldn't change until *Buena Vista Social Club*, which brought together some of Cuba's greatest older talent to celebrate son. Most of them had ended their careers, and were living in obscurity when the opportunity came knocking. The late Compay Segundo, now in his nineties, proved to be a charismatic figure, but all the major figures involved with the record had their own magic. Ibrahim Ferrer, who'd been supplementing his pension by shining shoes and selling lottery tickets, proved to be a remarkable voice and a quick study. Omara Portuondo, who'd been a star in the 1950s, had lost very little of her voice, and now-deceased Ruben González, who'd hardly touched a piano in years, quickly found his touch, in spite of arthritis. In fact, he more than found his touch; once sessions were finished, the crew took two more days to record a solo album for González. It wasn't long before both Ferrer and Portuondo were also recording their own albums, while Segundo signed a contract and recorded for another label.

Buena Vista Social Club was the kind of phenomenon no one could have predicted. The music was blatantly nostalgic, but it somehow struck a chord around the world, selling several million copies. The troupe toured, and Wim Wenders's movie was also a hit with audiences. In the wake of all this came the Cuban explosion.

Suddenly, record store shelves were filled with product from Cuba. Some of it was good, with powerful bands like ¡Cubanismo! pushing Cuban trumpet playing further. So while the flood did give access to music by them, the old doo-wop band Los Zafiros, the Afro-Cuban All Stars, and some others, it also brought forth plenty of lesser work.

It has, however, helped open the door for Cuban hip-hop. Though much of the style is still developing, Orishas (who are based in Europe, not Cuba) have found some success, and others seem set to follow them.

Mexico: The fixed image of Mexican music is mariachis in sombreros and heavily embroidered clothes. However, that's just one part of the tradition—and it's far from being representative. You can also find the ranchera, the romanticized style, norteño (Tex-Mex), and many more.

More than anything else, ranchera is the music that moves Mexicans; if there's one music that crosses all the barriers in the country, this is it. The name, derived from the word for *farm*, connotes a simpler, rural time, a harking back in Mexican history. But it's always been urban music, written and performed in the cities. Highly melodramatic, with vivid full orchestrations, it's music for singers, who really do make the most of it. It is interesting that the field has been equally divided between men and women; Lucha Reyes and José Alfredo Jiménez are two of the biggest names of the twentieth century (Jiménez was also a renowned ranchera composer). Coincidentally, both died tragically. They've been succeeded by singers like Vicente Fernández (perhaps the greatest living ranchera singer) and his son Alejandro, along with divas such as Astrid Haddad, who's developed into a fine singer of the style.

Norteño (also called Tejano) is most popular in the north of Mexico, as the name implies. Originally a regional, guitar-based music, it was revolutionized by the accordion. The instrument was actually introduced by nineteenth-century German settlers in Texas, who brought it from their homeland, along with the polka. Within a few years both had become the heart of norteño. The Jimenez family has been at the center of the accordion tradition; Santiago Jimenez was a pioneer of accordion norteño, and his sons, Santiago Jr. and Flaco, have carried on the tradition. Flaco developed a reputation for his solo career and his work with the Texas Tornados supergroup.

Part of norteño, although it's also a stand-alone genre, is the corrido. Essentially a folk ballad commemorating an event or a person, in recent years it's been superseded by the violent narcocorridos, tales of drug smugglers, generally involving plenty of bloodshed, and somewhat like gangsta rap (in fact, in many western U.S. states, Mexican and Mexican-American teenagers listen almost exclusively to gangsta rap and narcocorridos). Their content has made them the butt of much criticism, but the popularity is undiminished.

And no one sings them like Los Tigres del Norte. Since the 1970s they've been a major force, one of the top Mexican groups (although they actually live in California). They've made a few changes to the traditional style, but their music is very obviously norteño, with the accordion well out in the front.

In their wake have come the bandas, mixing norteño with the brass band style that's long been prevalent in villages all over Mexico. It's become a popular style, especially with the older generation.

Regional music is still very much alive across the country. In Veracruz, for example, the harp is a common instrument, whose leading proponent, Graciana Silva, brings an easy beauty to the instrument, with gloriously light melodies. Rural Oaxaco, with its Xapotec native culture, has found a champion in Mexican-American singer Lila Downs; she's performed some glowing arrangements of the songs, in addition to other music from Mexico. And Jalisco was the home of the mariachis, who have become a visual and musical Mexican symbol. There's a long-established mariachi repertoire, but they've mostly sung ranchera music, the trademark trumpets becoming a part of the sound only after the harp was no longer used.

Inevitably, the younger generation has been influenced by music from north of the border, although the best bands have put their own twist on it. Maldita Vecindad began their career in the 1980s, never aping bands from the United States, but instead finding their own rock sound with its Mexican roots. More recently, Café Tacuba made an impression with the alternative audience on both sides of the border. Los de Abajo also keep their sound very rooted in Mexican music, adding touches of ska, and topping everything off with very political lyrics.

Canada: One of the most obvious things about Canada is that there's no single Canadian musical expression. From Cape Breton in the east to the Inuit of the far north, it's a mishmash of different cultures—much the same as many Western countries, really. The difference, perhaps, is that the various voices are extremely well defined and confident.

The East Coast scene, as it's been called, has received plenty of attention over the past decade, although its roots go back more than a century. The area was largely settled by Scots and Irish immigrants, with Cape Breton in particular becoming home to a large Scots community who brought their music, especially fiddle music, with them. The rugged area's relative isolation meant that the tradition remained intact, with few outside influences—in some respects purer than back in Scotland.

Buddy MacMaster was the zenith of the Cape Breton tradition, although in his day it was largely confined to the Cape itself. It was the Rankin Family who first took the music nationwide, although their approach was through traditional song, rather than playing, and toned down for wider appeal.

MacMaster's niece, Natalie MacMaster, was the first outstanding Cape Breton fiddler to make an impact outside her home. After two self-released cassettes, she won an East Coast Music Award for the very rootsy *Fit as a Fiddle* in 1992, before going on to an international career.

If Natalie MacMaster offers the respectable face of tradition, another fiddler, Ashley MacIsaac, is its wild side. His 1995 debut, *Hi! How Are You Today?* brought Cape Breton crashing into the end of the twentieth century, mixing in electric guitars and hyperspeed playing, tempered only by the airy "Sleepy Maggie," featuring the Gaelic vocals of Mary Jane Lamond.

Following her exposure with MacIsaac, Lamond has forged a career for herself as a singer of great voice and intelligence. With Gaelic vocals, her albums have been relentlessly experimental, employing touches of ambient, hip-hop, and even New Age music. But the heart of it all has been the tradition that's her heritage, and she treats it with great respect.

Québec, of course, is Francophone Canada, and it has its own long-standing traditions dating back to the original French immigrants. Those traditions have tended to remain very much on the folk level, though, not finding an audience outside the province. In fact, few Québecois musicians have been able to translate their music beyond the language lines. For La Bottine Souriante (The Smiling Boot) it took more than twenty years of playing before they were able to become internationally known. Their take on the traditional has emphasized the beat—a kind of folk-rock—but it's only since they brought in other elements, like Cajun music and added a horn section, that they've found real success. On the other hand, Matapat have kept the music stripped down and acoustic, even including step dancing. Born from the band Ad Vielle Que Pourra, they've established themselves on the festival circuit across North America and Europe, never compromising their sound.

The First Nations, as native Canadians are known, have long had a champion in former Band guitarist Robbie

Robertson, who's part Mohawk. He's explored his heritage over the course of several albums and encouraged younger talent like Kashtin, an Innu duo from northern Québec. The best-known First Nation artist remains Buffy Sainte-Marie, a Cree Indian from Saskatchewan who came to prominence in the 1960s. Several of her songs, like "Now That the Buffalo's Gone" and the controversial "Soldier Blue," dealt with the plight and trials of native peoples. Jerry Alfred, of the Selkirk group in the Yukon, has lived up to his shamanic status on his albums. Singing in his native tongue, and backed by the Medicine Band, he creates soundscapes that are strikingly similar to the modern music of the Nordic Sami people.

Throughout Canada, immigrants of all kinds are hanging on to and often reinventing their music. You'll find them mostly in the big cities, like Toronto and Vancouver, and several excellent performers, like African guitarist Alapha Yaya Diallo (who's based on the West Coast) have emerged onto the international scene.

United States: In world music terms, the United States might be the most complex nation on earth. Inside its borders you can hear almost everything. The music it's birthed—jazz, blues, country, bluegrass, Cajun, zydeco, and gospel—all have their roots elsewhere; it's been in the way the pieces have come together that something new has been created. Perhaps the only pure form is Native American music, but even much of that has been co-opted by New Age sounds over the past two decades.

The history of the United States over the past four centuries has centered on immigration, whether forced or voluntary. It's been a haven for the poor and hungry from elsewhere, a golden land of opportunity, at least, for those who came willingly.

One result of immigration, and the westward expansion of the immigrant population, was the forced movement of native tribes. Eventually pushed onto reservations, often far from where they'd originally lived, native culture was trampled and demeaned by the white majority for many years. It's only since the late 1960s that native pride has helped a resurgence of all the traditions and the culture. It's most evident at powwows held around the country, where the signing, drumming, and dancing celebrate the ceremonies and the tradition. Powwows can be found throughout the United States in the summer. There are recordings of them, but it's something best experienced in the flesh.

Native American performers have finally achieved some prominence, emerging quite forcefully from the underground. There are groups like the very traditional Black Lodge Singers, singer/songwriters such as John Trudell, Joanne Shenandoah, Rita Coolidge, and Bill Miller, and extremely political rock groups like Blackfire, who still manage to hew to the heart of their culture.

The flute has long been an important native instrument in native music, originally used for love and courting songs. Artists like R. Carlos Nakai and Kevin Locke have helped move it, if not into the musical mainstream, then at least to the point at which it's a readily recognized instrument. Nakai in particular has received widespread praise as a master of the instrument and one who's put it into many different settings, from New Age to classical.

Cajun and zydeco is the music of Louisiana and has been for a couple of centuries, since the British forced the French out of Nova Scotia and they had to find a new home. In many ways they're two sides of the same coin: Cajun is the white tradition, with very strong French roots, whereas zydeco comes more from the African American past, bringing in a bit more R&B to the equation. However, they share so much (and harking back, it was common to find black musicians playing white dances, although they weren't allowed in the same room) that separating the two sometimes becomes difficult, and certainly if you go back fifty or seventy-five years.

As with so many folk forms, they began with the house dances, where the fiddle was the predominant instrument, followed by the accordion, which was introduced in the early part of the twentieth century. Cajun music made its recorded debut around the same time as early country music and proved to be a big regional seller. "Jolie Blon," probably the most familiar of all Cajun songs, dates from this time. It's been revisited so often, and by so many artists, that's it's become *the* classic of the genre.

For a few decades, there were attempts to eradicate the French culture of Louisiana, but none succeeded. The language and the Cajun music remained, although many years would pass before French became accepted in schools again. In fact, much of the great Cajun music dates from this time, when people like Iry LeJeune made their mark.

The Cajun music most people know is more recent, the product of groups like the Balfa Brothers or the Savoy-Doucet Band (Michael Doucet is also a member of Beausoleil, another excellent Cajun band). And it's really the groups, incorporating guitar along with fiddle and accordion (and sometimes percussion or drums, too), that have become known, leading the revival of Cajun music, usually playing acoustically, and covering the great songs from the repertoire.

The problem with that is that it tends to make the music static and turn it into a museum piece. But some younger, more iconoclastic artists have come along. Steve Riley and the Mamou Playboys started out quite traditionally, singing only in French and using acoustic instruments; lately they've added original material in English, and many other instrumental textures. Their music is unmistakably Cajun, but also unashamedly modern. Zachary Richard, who's been involved with Louisiana music for decades, mixes up rock and Cajun music on his albums.

Zydeco springs from black roots, but it's historically informed by the same French music that became Cajun. Certainly until the 1950s, there was plenty of crossover between the two styles. Accordionists like Amédé Ardoin (who played with a white fiddler, Dennis McGee) and fiddlers like Canray Fontenot (generally acknowledged as one of the greatest to come from Louisiana) had great influence on white as well as black musicians.

It wasn't until after World War II that zydeco (the word is thought to derive from the French word for "beans," *haricots*) in its modern form began to emerge. The washboard added syncopated rhythm, and the structure of the music began leaning closer to blues and R&B. Before long, the King of Zydeco began to emerge. Clifton Chenier souped up the music, playing it a little faster and using bigger accordions to achieve a larger sound. It was immediately successful, and Chenier became a fixture on the circuit of zydeco clubs that exists throughout rural Louisiana and Texas. He did manage to break out into bigger things toward the end of his career, finding national fame.

For many years, Chenier (who's been succeeded by his son, C. J.) was zydeco's leading name. But there were many challengers, including the late Boozoo Chavis, who stuck closer to the music's roots; Buckwheat Zydeco; and Queen Ida, who's based not in Louisiana, but in the San Francisco area.

What *Buena Vista Social Club* was to Cuban music—a breath of new life and interest—the soundtrack to *O Brother Where*

Art Thou? was for bluegrass. It brought the music back into fashion, and made household names of some of the old-timers, like Ralph Stanley, who'd been playing the music without compromise for years.

Although its roots lie in the raw country folk music of Appalachia, bluegrass owes its existence to one man—Bill Monroe. Beginning in the late 1930s, he put together the Blue Grass Boys, with fiddle, banjo, and guitar and himself at the front, playing mandolin and singing. They built on the country sound pioneered by artists like the Carter Family and the string bands of the 1920s. He trained his musicians to play fast and with discipline and introduced baritone and tenor harmonies to accompany his "high lonesome" singing.

Others imitated him. Lester Flatt and Earl Scruggs, who'd played with Monroe, started their own, successful band in the late 1940s. Stanley, who's always played what he called "mountain music," became a force from the mid-1950s on.

Through the decades, the music has developed and grown, and even spawned the more contemporary newgrass style. But it remained on the fringes of country music, seen as a more traditional form, and left behind when country reinvented itself as "new country" and began attracting a mass audience.

The reemergence of bluegrass follows the rise of the alt-country, or Americana, movement, a reaction against country's blatant commerciality, and a retreat to country songs with meaning. But not even that prepared people for the remarkable success of the music for *O Brother Where Are Thou?* It sold literally millions of copies in the United States alone, topping the country charts and bringing Ralph Stanley's trademark songs, "O Death" and "I Am a Man of Constant Sorrow," into the mainstream of American music.

* * *

Polka has never captured the attention that bluegrass has, but it remains an important underpinning of the American roots music scene, brought to the country by immigrants from central Europe.

The music's origin is legendary. Supposedly created during the 1830s in Czech Bohemia by a girl named Anna Slezakova, within a decade the dance, performed in quick double-time, was popular throughout Europe, and even in America, where it was danced by the upper classes.

That changed with increasing Czech and German immigration. The people brought their polka with them to cities like Buffalo, Chicago, and Milwaukee, and across the Midwest and into Texas, where it influenced Mexican norteño music (in Latin countries, traces of the polka can be heard in Brazilian forró and the cumbia in Colombia).

The first U.S. polka recording came in 1903, and by 1912 several record labels were releasing polkas, boosted by the popularity of ballroom dancing. But polka's breakthrough into mass consciousness had to wait until the mid 1930s, when Will Glahe's "The Beer Barrel Polka" was a massive hit, with the version by the Andrews Sisters in 1939 being even bigger.

By then, polka was firmly entrenched in many places, especially in the Midwest, a scene with its own stars like Frankie Yankovic, the "Polka King" (and father of "Weird" Al), and "Whoope John" Wilfart, whose popularity was greatest in the 1940s and 1950s. Lawrence Welk helped turn polka into something recognized across the country by homogenizing it for his TV show; but at a roots level, the style could be a stirring, raw sound.

Different styles of polka emerged in different areas, and even when rock 'n' roll came of age in the 1960s, polka stayed alive in dances at church halls and V.F.W. posts across the Rust Belt and beyond.

But it never died and indeed has enjoyed a revival since the 1980s (since 1986 there has been a Grammy for polka), with a mix of longtime and young artists preserving and expanding the music. Brave Combo and Polkacide have emerged as one of the most adventurous of the new outfits, mixing polka with many other styles on their releases. The prolific Jimmy Sturr is the current monarch of the more traditional style.

Klezmer, that particularly Jewish music, started life in central Europe, where Yiddish was the common tongue and Jewish and Romany musicians played the music side by side. But it flowered in the United States, especially around New York, where immigrant musicians had more freedom than they'd enjoyed in the old country. In addition to becoming a vital form on its own, one that has enjoyed a renaissance over the past two decades, it became one of the streams that influenced jazz; listen to the clarinet of swing king Benny Goodman, and you can hear klezmer.

Klezmer musicians, or *klezmorim*, played at weddings, dances, and all manner of occasions; the violin was the principal instrument, although clarinet took its place during the nineteenth century. All across central Europe where the Ashkenazi Jews lived, klezmer was the sound, playing versions of popular and folk dances, with Jewish and Gypsy musicians often swapping places, depending on availability.

In the decades around the turn of the twentieth century, millions of Jews left Europe for the New World. For some it was the chance of a better life; others were escaping the pogroms that promised violence and an early death.

It wasn't long before American record companies were releasing klezmer music to satisfy the musical appetites of the new immigrants. New stars were made, people like clarinetists Dave Tarras and Naftule Brandwein, who sold plenty of records and made a living from their music—something they'd never expected on entering the country. The concentration of population was around New York, which is where the music developed, gradually melding into jazz. As the immigrant population assimilated, and their children moved to the suburbs, the music seemed to die.

It might well have stayed that way, but an adventurous younger generation began reviving the music in the mid-1970s. Bands like the Klezmatics and the Klezmorim began playing the old tunes, often bringing them up to date with new ideas. Some, such as Hasidic New Wave, mixed klezmer with free jazz to offer a thrillingly different take.

It is interesting that the American klezmer revival kick-started interest in the music in Europe, where some musicians have begun rediscovering their Jewish heritage; sadly, so many of Europe's Jews were wiped out during World War II. As a general rule, the European bands tend to stick closer to the music's roots, while the American bands often use klezmer as little more than a jumping-off point. Klezmatics leader, trumpeter Frank London (who's also involved in Hasidic New Wave and several other groups), has perhaps stretched the genre the furthest, with some radical ideas that often change the face of klezmer, while still managing to remain true to its tradition.

Modern klezmer hasn't recaptured its Jewish audience, however. Instead, its appeal is partly to a world music audience and also to those who enjoy the cutting edge of jazz.

Klezmer isn't the only music to start life outside the United States but to flourish within its borders. Salsa, too, found its fullest expression in America. But it was the culmination of a Latin music scene that had been bubbling since the late 1940s. Machito was the first to break through, but it was Tito

Puente who became the big star of the 1950s, riding the crazes for the mambo and the cha-cha-cha with ease. A powerful timbale player, he'd been involved with music since he was a child growing up in New York, and was a more than able bandleader. His sessions at Birdland in the 1950s became legendary.

Interest in Latin music waned during the 1960s, although Santana piqued some curiosity with their first two releases, where rock and Latin worked perfectly together (especially on a cover of Puente's "Oye Como Va"). But they weren't really serving the needs of a growing Latino population, who felt excluded from rock.

There was some music to serve them, by the likes of Willie Colón, who covered Cuban son and Puerto Rican classics on the Fania label. Then, at the start of the 1970s, Fania put together a team of crack New York–based Latin musicians, the Fania All Stars, who began playing around the city to great acclaim. Their music—a grab-bag of Latin styles with the emphasis on a fiery, percussive edge, excellent solos, and powerful singing—was an instant winner, to the point at which they could fill the city's biggest venues on a regular basis.

Salsa, as the music came to be called (the name translates as "sauce"), had plenty to draw on. Not only were there Cuban styles but also Puerto Rican, Colombian, and Dominican—almost every danceable Latin rhythm was fair game. And the Fania All Stars used them all, mixing and matching to create new permutations. They also brought along plenty of new stars, such as the late expatriate Cuban singer Celia Cruz, who quickly became the Queen of Salsa, and Panamanian Rubén Blades, who has gone on to become a major figure in American Latin music (and Panamanian politics).

Inevitably, salsa became the music of Latins in the United States, at least until the advent of Latin pop in the 1990s, which largely developed out of the Miami salsa scene, where salsa and pop merged—Gloria Estefan, with her producer husband Emilio, were pioneers of the new Latin pop.

With the rise of the less hardcore Latin pop, salsa has faded from the scene, although it can still be found in New York clubs. Ironically, while it's faded as live music, it's become more popular on record for the salsa dancing craze that's been in vogue across the country.

Rubén Blades has remained an important figure in the music. A Harvard-trained lawyer, he's introduced political elements into the lyrics, and pushed the boundaries of salsa by working with rock musicians. He's also stood for the presidency of his native Panama.

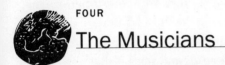

The Musicians

I t's impossible to list all the performers of world music, or even the ones whose music has seen international release and acceptance; the list would fill up this entire book and more.

Even defining a major performer is problematic. Someone could be venerated in an obscure style at home but utterly unknown outside his or her own country. On the other hand, a star in a style like Latin pop might be almost a household name but shouldn't be included here because the style is pop, not world music.

Everyone included here has made an important, often vital, contribution to music. They've established reputations from performances and recordings. In some instances, their careers have stretched across several decades. Often, they've changed the course of music within their own regions, to a greater or lesser degree.

It's the performers who make the music and convince the

audience. They possess the ability and the charisma. They also have the innate belief in what they're doing, whether it's moving farther along a well-traveled path or breaking new ground. And they carry the people with them—they make others believe in them.

There's no template of what a great world music performer should be. Different musical styles have different requirements, and, as the world grows smaller, the fusions of different elements have their own needs and stars.

This chapter highlights artists from every corner of the world who've made a real difference to music. Most of them have music readily available in the United States, although some might be harder to find than others. But the search will always be worthwhile.

Politics and world music unfortunately have to go hand in hand. Some of these artists have been government-approved heroes at home, even continuing to enjoy a regular existence in their native villages and cities, while others have had to flee for their lives. It's a reminder that art of any kind doesn't exist in a vacuum; it's part of living, with all the joys and sorrows that involves.

Africa, North Africa, Middle East

King Sunny Ade (b. 1946): King Sunny Ade deserves his crown. He's still the biggest name in Nigerian juju music, and the one who took it to a global level. Born to Nigerian royalty— which meant nothing—by his mid-teens he was already a professional musician, forming his first band, the Green Spots, in 1967. In 1974 he launched his own label, changed his group's name to the African Beats, and has since moved from strength to strength. He's been a constant innovator, most noted for adding pedal steel guitar to his band's expansive (over twenty players!) lineup. In 1982 Island Records tried to position Ade as a star to follow the late Bob Marley, and *Juju Music* appeared to critical acclaim but only moderate sales. However, from that toehold he's built a dedicated international audience. After a lull in the late 1980s and early 1990s, he's experienced a creative rebirth on the world music scene, which has welcomed him back. In Nigeria he's a major cultural force, head of the Musicians Union, a club owner, and major charitable contributor.

Cesaria Evora (b. 1941): The barefoot diva, as she's known, has become the soul of Cape Verde. Evora began singing when she was young and struggled to make a living singing in Cape Verde clubs through her twenties, before taking time off to raise a family. When she returned to music in 1985, she was invited to Portugal by a women's association to record her debut album. However, her lived-in voice and local morna style didn't take off; it wasn't until three years later that she returned to the studio, this time in Paris where she made *La Diva Aux Pieds Nus*. While not a huge success, it found favor with the expatriate Cape Verdean community, and her next two albums continued the upward swing. It was 1992's *Miss Perfumado* that was her big breakthrough, its aching tone catching European and American ears, the music (like the islands themselves) halfway between Africa and Brazil. Since finding fame on an international level, Evora has received three Grammy nominations and has been acknowledged as one of the great voices of world music.

Franco (1938–1989): Born Francois Luambo Makiadi in the Congolese village of Sona-Bata, Franco would go on to earn the nickname "The Sorcerer of the Guitar," a standout in a continent that's produced some of the world's most remarkable instrumentalists. At the age of ten he'd mastered a homemade guitar, and by the time he was fifteen he was making his recording debut. But it was as the leader of OK Jazz that he made his reputation. An excellent singer and writer as well as guitarist, he wrote songs that were personal observations and conduits of information—and that were lapped up by the public. However, the state didn't always agree. Several of his records were banned by the Mobutu regime of Zaire, and Franco saw the inside of a jail a few times. His music became an empire to the extent that, for a while, he ran two versions of his band, one based in Europe, the other in Kinshasa. A giant of a man, whose top weight was over three hundred pounds, he remained a constantly inventive and fluid player. One of his most renowned pieces was among his last: "Attention Na Sida," ("Beware of AIDS") from 1987 came when he was becoming sick with the disease that would kill him. Prolific, and always happy to be in the studio, he left an extensive legacy of music. But more than that, he remained a musical rock through change, launching the careers of a number of artists and rarely letting the magic falter.

Salif Keita (b. 1949): Keita is the name of the ancient aristocratic line in the Mande Empire, and aristocrats didn't sing; socially, it was simply unacceptable. But Salif Keita could sing, and wanted to, which was a guarantee of family conflict in his village of Djoliba in Mali. Keita was also born albino, which in Africa made him a social outcast. Even his father had little contact with him. After training as a teacher to please his family, he risked their wrath by going to Bamako to become a singer, for which his father disowned him. After working with the Rail Band and Les Ambassadeurs, with whom he cut the classic track "Mandjou," he ventured out as a solo performer. With his debut, 1987's *Soro*, he hit an immediate home run, fusing Mande and modern music. Making his home in Paris, he continued to record and tour. Nicknamed "The Golden Voice of Africa" for his remarkably pure, high vocals, his career seemed to veer between high and low points through the 1990s (with the very mainstream, jazzy *Papa* as a nadir). However, after moving back to Bamako, he returned to his roots with *Moffou* in 2002, a largely acoustic record that showed he'd lost none of his range or stunning talent.

Khaled (b. 1960): Khaled Hadj Bahim was born in the Algerian town of Oran, the center of raï. By the time he was fourteen, Khaled could already play several instruments. While still a young teen he released "Trigh Lycée," a song about playing truant and chasing girls, and it made him into an overnight sensation. With his band, the Five Stars, he began playing the raï circuit of weddings and seedy clubs as well as recording cassettes as often as possible. A collaboration with innovative producer Rachid Baba Ahmed in the 1980s gave "Cheb" Khaled (as he was called) a new, poppier sound, taking his music to an entirely new level and letting his powerful, raw voice really shine. Moving to Paris in 1986, he spent a few years establishing himself on a broader stage. Not until 1993's *N'ssi N'ssi* did he begin to break through, and since then his popularity has grown, to the point at which he's become an icon among Algerian expatriates and one of the great voices of modern world music. Justifiably called the King of Raï, he continues to tour, and his records still take chances.

Um Kulthum (1904–1975): Egyptian Um Kulthum was a country girl who showed remarkable talent as a singer, enough for her family to move to Cairo to give her an opportunity at fame. But it took coaching, as her rustic ways and vocal style just weren't sophisticated enough. She took instruction in diction and literature from the poet Ahmad Rami and emerged the perfect star. She made her first recordings in 1926, amazing everyone with her command of complex melodic system and the yearning, melismatic quality of her voice. Soon the best composers were writing for her, and when Egyptian radio began broadcasting in 1934, her fame spread across the entire country, then eventually the whole Middle East, which would come to a standstill as people crowded around radios to hear her monthly concerts. A strong supporter of self-rule, she released several patriotic songs when Nasser came to power in 1952. During the 1960s, her focus changed to more romantic songs, as she began working with other composers, especially Mohamed Abdel Wahab. Her final concert appearance came in 1972, and she died in February 1975. For the funeral of the "Mother of the Arabs," four million people lined the streets of Cairo.

Fela Kuti (1938–1997): The last thing Fela Kuti's parents wanted was for him to become a musician. Born in Abeokuta, a small Nigerian town north of Lagos, Fela Anikalupo Ransome-Kuti had been sent off to London to study medicine. Instead, without telling his mother or father, he studied music, but quickly tired of European composers and formed his first band. He returned to Nigeria in 1963 and began fusing the American soul music he'd heard in England with the local highlife style. That was the birth of Afrobeat, a hybrid he'd continue to develop, with its seamless mix of funk and West African rhythms. In 1969, Kuti and his band arrived in the United States, eventually being deported—their residence wasn't exactly legal. Back in Lagos again, Kuti began his own nightclub, the Shrine, and continued his volatile musical path. Speaking out loudly on behalf of the poor and opposing corruption and the lingering effects of colonialism brought him into almost constant conflict with the government. In 1977 his compound was burned, and a few years later he was sentenced to jail (he served only one year). But his music never stopped. A prolific recorder, he made over seventy albums during his career, before succumbing to the AIDS in 1997.

Femi Kuti (b. 1962): On Fela Kuti's death, his son Femi, also Nigerian, took over the leadership of his band. The saxophonist had stepped into the breach before when Fela was sick or in jail. But although he's largely kept to the Afrobeat blueprint laid down over a couple of decades, Femi Kuti's gone on to make it his own. An ardent AIDS activist, Kuti prefers illustration and persuasion to confrontation in his lyrics—and he tends to sing in English, rather than his father's pidgin, bringing him closer to a global audience. A stunning, energetic live performer, he's brought in more jazz elements and isn't afraid to lessen the length of the songs, understanding that brevity can often have its own impact. Through three albums he's fully grown into his own vision, with 2001's *Fight to Win* showing a particular brilliance. The piece "97" stands as a tribute to his father and sister, who died the same year. An accomplished instrumentalist, Kuti's making the new Afrobeat into a style that's viable in the West in the new millennium.

Baaba Maal (b. 1959?): Baaba Maal comes from the Fulani people in the north of Senegal. Born in Podor, close to the Mauritanian border, he studied music at the Conservatory in Dakar before winning a scholarship to Paris. On his return, he teamed up with his family griot, Mansour Seck (who still plays with Maal, although he's released several albums of his own). Together they recorded the acoustic *Djam Leelii* before forming Daane Lenol (Voice of the People) and upping both volume and technical quotient. But his musical career has tended to be schizophrenic, alternating between electric and acoustic albums. His 1994 disc, *Firin' in Fouta,* mixed Senegalese sounds with Celtic music, hip-hop, and ragga to give his greatest commercial impact, while *Nomad Soul,* four years later, used avant-garde icon Brian Eno among its producers. In 2001 he seemed to instigate the recent acoustic roots Zeitgeist of African music with the disarming live disc *Missing You (Mi Yeewnii),* which showcased his soaring voice to great effect. Eclectic and adventurous, he's always followed his own muse without a thought to fad or fashion.

Miriam Makeba (b. 1932): Possibly no South African musician, or even any South African woman, has a name as recognizable as Miriam Makeba. She was the first African to win a Grammy (in 1959) and to score a U.S. hit ("Pata-Pata" in 1967). She sang at the birthday tribute to President Kennedy in 1961 and at the birth of the Organization of African Unity in 1963. She received the Dag Hammerskjöld Peace Prize in 1968 for her outspoken views opposing Apartheid. After starting her professional life singing with the Manhattan Brothers, she formed the female harmony group the Skylarks before going on to take the lead in the musical *King Kong,* which brought her to Broadway and whose soundtrack LP won her the Grammy. She stayed in the United States, marrying Black Panther leader Stokely Carmichael. That political connection hurt her career, and she moved to Guinea, where she served as the country's delegate to the United Nations. Along the way she married for a second time, to expatriate countryman Hugh Masekela, and managed to maintain a musical career, including appearing on the *Graceland* tour and performing with Odetta and Nina Simone, while recording a series of albums. She returned to South Africa in 1990, but a decade would pass before she'd resume recording, issuing the very rooted and celebratory *Homeland* in 2000.

Thomas Mapfumo (b. 1945): Born in the Zimbabwean village of Marondera, Mapfumo started out playing covers of Western rock (in copyright bands, as they were called), but found his sound in the late 1970s after he began singing in Shona. His incendiary songs so incensed the authorities that he spent three months in jail, being released only after agreeing to perform at a political rally. However, he claimed he'd been unable to write new material while incarcerated and ended up playing the material that had provoked his arrest in the first place! After the country's independence, he became an icon for the people, unafraid to speak out against corruption in the new regime. His countrymen named him Zimbabwe's Arts, Literature, Culture Person of the Century, even as some of his singles were banned from radio for their attacks on leader Robert Mugabe. The government's tactic then was to charge him with receiving stolen property, forcing him to leave the country and settle in the United States, although he returns home to perform regularly, at some personal risk. He's continued to be prolific, not only experimenting with his trademark "electric mbira" style but also going unplugged at times. In addition, he's detoured to work with avant-garde jazz musician Wadada Leo Smith.

Youssou N'Dour (b. 1959): Possibly the best-known figure in African music, Senegal's N'Dour has been universally lauded for his remarkable voice. Half-griot (on his mother's side), he has the natural wail of the caste tempered with a remarkable range and sensitivity. Starting out as a teenager singing with the successful, heavily Cuban-influenced Star Band in Dakar, he broke away with several musicians to form Super Étoile de Dakar. Remarkably innovative, their music was more African, ushering in the incredibly popular mbalax style. By the early 1980s, N'Dour was beginning to attract global attention, which would be consolidated later in the decade when he toured with Peter Gabriel and released his first international album, *The Lion*. Other albums followed, but it wasn't until 1994 that he managed a hit single, "7 Seconds," a duet with British singer/rapper Neneh Cherry. His voice and the quality of his mbalax material has already assured his revered position, but since the mid-1990s, he's retreated a little on the international front, where his albums have sometimes been criticized for attempting to second-guess Western tastes. At home he opened the state-of-the-art Xippi recording studio and has helped the careers of several Senegalese artists. He continues to release cassettes for the home market on his own Jololi label, while making different records for the global market. In 2002 he seemed to experience something of a creative rebirth with *Nothing's in Vain* (*Coono du réér*), and followed in 2004 with *Egypt*, an adventurous testament to his Islamic faith.

Kazem Al-Saher (b. 1961): Kazem Al-Saher found success in Iraq through the back door. Although he trained at the Baghdad Institute, he found his own work rejected by all the producers he approached. However, he made a video for his song "Ladghat El Hayya" (The Snake Bite), and he managed to sneak it on to national television in 1987, at the tail end of the Iran-Iraq war. The song was banned after he refused to alter its controversial lyrics, but that served only to make Al-Saher more popular. But after establishing himself with a pop song he changed tack, and with 1989's epic *La Ya Sadiki* (No, My Friend) established himself as a contemporary Iraqi composer of note. He finally left the country in 1993, and since then his career has blossomed, both as pop star and serious singer and composer. He's won a UNICEF award and is possibly the only Iraqi to perform for the U.S. Congress in the post–Gulf War years. While the source of his music is indubitably Iraqi, he's stayed abreast of contemporary developments, and his only American album to date, *The Impossible Love*, featured a Transglobal Underground remix of "La Titnahad." When he attempted a return to his native land in the late 1990s he was shot, although not seriously wounded. He toured the United States in early 2003.

Super Rail Band (founded 1969): Formed to play in the buffet of Bamako's railroad station in Mali, the Super Rail Band hasn't just been a crucible for great talent like Salif Keita and Mory Kante, it's become one of the very best groups to emerge from West Africa. Led by guitarist Djelimady Tounkara, whose fluid style is a group trademark, they've taken Mande music to a new level. They briefly disbanded in the 1970s over a wage dispute, but since reforming they've gone on to international acclaim, following a slow period in the 1980s. These days they frequently tour Europe and the United States. Surprisingly, however, they haven't released many recordings in the West.

Tarika (founded 1993): Tarika (which translates simply as "The Group"), led by female singer Hanitra Rasoanaivo and her sister, Norosoa, started life in 1983, when Hanitra (pronounced *ansch*) translated for the Englishmen recording on Madagascar for a pair of Globestyle compilations. The sisters formed a band, Tarika Sammy, with local musician Sammy Andraimanahirana, eventually going their own way as just

Tarika and featuring the indigenous valiha, marovany, and kabosy within their five-piece band. It was impossible to make a living solely from music in Madagascar—indeed, it was unheard of, since music was something one did just as a part of life—so they relocated to London and began touring and playing relentlessly. Their second album, *Son Egal*, won wide praise for its discussion of a 1947 rebellion, when islanders attempted to throw off French colonial shackles and the Europeans reacted by bringing in Senegalese troops. The record featured members of Baaba Maal's band from Senegal, healing old wounds. *D* saw them covering old Malagasy dance hits from the 1960s and 1970s, and *Soul Makassar* explored the Indonesian heritage of the Malagasy people. Never short of ambition, Tarika have the energy and technique to back it up, and both performances and discs have marked them as the most important contemporary band to emerge from Madagascar.

Ali Farka Touré (b. 1939): Born in northern Mali, on the edge of the Sahara, Ali Farka Touré is a guitarist who connects the dots between American blues and West Africa. Based in the village of Niafunké, where he still farms (and uses his record royalties to improve conditions for the villagers), he first came to prominence in Mali from some 1970s radio sessions. But it wasn't until his startling eponymous international debut in 1988 that the musical connection between the African and the American was so obviously shown (although Touré was a long-time fan of bluesman John Lee Hooker, whose work his monochordal style resembles). Building on that start, Touré has released an impressive series of albums, including a 1994 duet disc with Ry Cooder, *Talking Timbuktu*, that won a Grammy. His last release was 1999's *Niafunké*, and, according to rumor, he has now largely retired from music.

Asia

Sheila Chandra (b. 1965): Although she started as an actress on the British school soap opera *Grange Hill*, Anglo-Asian artist Sheila Chandra's heart was in singing. She teamed up with writer/producer Steve Coe to form Monsoon, who had a big British hit in 1982 with the Indian-inflected "Ever So Lonely." After Monsoon ended, Chandra began working as a solo artist, pushing the boundaries of what she'd learned as a singer, although she was still just a teenager; in fact, at the age of twenty, she took a two-year break from singing to research music to try to discover what she wanted of herself as an artist, returning with *Roots and Wings*. On that album, drones became an important factor in her sound, in addition to exploring and interweaving the vocal traditions of different cultures with just a single voice. She developed the style over three more bravura albums, with *ABoneCroneDrone* being particularly adventurous, working purely around drones and their harmonics. After that she developed chronic rhenitis, which was finally diagnosed and cured, and she eased her way back to singing by making two wildly experimental EPs with the Ganges Orchestra (actually Coe, her life as well as musical partner). They were followed in 2001 by *This Sentence Is True*, which built on both the EP work and her previous albums and took them several steps further.

Zakir Hussain (b. 1951): Known for his brilliant tabla playing, India's Hussain is also virtuosic on all forms of Indian percussion. Born into a musical family (his father played tabla with Ravi Shankar), Hussain has extensively performed classical music, but his reputation has been made through his collaborations with others—such as his time in the Indo-jazz fusion band Shakti and his work with Mickey Hart in Planet Drum.

Hussain was just nineteen when he made his international debut, accompanying Shankar in New York. Within three years he was leading his own Tal Vadya Rhythm Band (which went through several name changes) and then pushing at the edge with Shakti. In 1992, he was a Grammy winner for the *Planet Drum* disc. A truly multifaceted performer, he's remained equally at home with both contemporary world fusions and classical music, a performer who's constantly pushing the barriers of his music wider and wider.

Huun-Huur-Tu (formed 1992): With their colorful robes and traditional instruments, Tuva's Huun-Huur-Tu offer a splendid sight onstage. Once they open their mouths and produce the remarkable, unearthly tones of throat singing, however, looks become irrelevant as the waves of sound overwhelm you. The group, originally named Kungurtuk, came together in 1992 when Alexander and Sayan Bapa, along with Albert Kuvezin and Kaigal-ol Khovalyg, left a state ensemble to concentrate on performing traditional Tuvan music. Changing their name to Huun-Huur-Tu (literally, "sun propeller"), they made their first visit to the United States in 1993, where they collaborated with such diverse talents as Frank Zappa, Ry Cooder, and the Chieftains. However, while the spectacular throat singing has helped make them a fixture on the world music festival and concert circuit, they do far more than just that. Much of their repertoire is made up of folk songs, using traditional instruments and "normal" voices that illustrate more of the facets of Tuva. Their four albums to date have been split between song and throat singing, with accomplished (but rarely mentioned) instrumental playing. Essentially, they bring together several different aspects of Tuvan music in a single package, offering a synthesis of the country but always emphasizing that loping rhythm of the horse, which seems almost second nature—as does the repeated lyrical imagery of horses in the songs.

Ali Akbar Khan (b. 1922): The master of the sarod, Ali Akbar Khan is as important a figure in north Indian classical music as his brother-in-law, Ravi Shankar. The virtuoso Yehudi Menuhin called him "the greatest musician in the world." Born in what's now Bangladesh to a renowned multi-instrumentalist with a lineage of court musicians, Khan was trained by his father from the age of three. In 1955, Menuhin invited him to appear in Europe and America, the first of many such trips he'd make. In 1967 he established the Ali Akbar College of Music in California—a companion to the one he'd founded eleven years earlier in India. While he's devoted a lot of his time to teaching, he's also been a dedicated performing and recording artist. Lauded for his both his sense of time and melody, he's made the sarod into one of the major instruments of the style.

Nusrat Fateh Ali Khan (1948–1997): Not just a great singer of devotional qawwali, Pakistan's Nusrat Fateh Ali Khan was one of the great voices of the twentieth century. He had the power to move audiences who didn't even understand a word he was singing, and his dazzling improvisations could stun listeners. Part of a six-hundrd-year-old family vocal tradition, Khan first recorded in Pakistan in 1973 and quickly became prodigious. During the 1980s he traveled abroad, and the recordings of his 1985 Paris concerts show the breadth and depth of his talent, both on the mystical qawwali texts and the lighter romantic poetry called ghazals. It was mostly thanks to his releases on the Real World label, however, that he was able to break through to the highest level of world music and fill concert halls around the globe. While devoted to his sacred songs, he continued to experiment, working with producer Michael Brook on a pair of wonderful sound-scaped records. He even duetted with Pearl Jam's Eddie Vedder on two songs for a movie soundtrack. Physically large, and suffering from diabetes, he was en route to the United States for a kidney transplant when he died of renal failure in London.

Wu Man (b. 1965): China's Wu Man is the woman who took the pipa, a type of lute, international. Born in Hangzhou, she began her musical training at age ten; she graduated from the Beijing's Central Conservatory of Music, being awarded the first-ever master's degree in pipa and then winning the first National Academic competition for Chinese Instruments. Perhaps the leading exponent of the Pudong school of pipa playing, she's become a globally recognized virtuoso on the instrument and helped introduce it to the West. While still playing traditional music for the instrument, she's remained open to taking it in new directions, collaborating with the New York New Music Consort and the groundbreaking Kronos Quartet and also championing the work of new Chinese composers.

She's an artist who has made her instrument recognized outside China, perhaps more in classical rather than in world music circles. But by preserving some of the traditional music for the pipa, she's performed an invaluable service for all who love music, period. She's recorded widely, both solo and with others, and is a member of Yo-Yo Ma's Silk Road Ensemble. She's a Bunting Fellow at the Radcliffe Institute of Harvard University and lives in Boston.

Ravi Shankar (b. 1920): Given his reputation on the sitar, it's perhaps hard to believe that India's Ravi Shankar hasn't devoted his entire life to the instrument. But he began his musical career as a dancer and, in fact, was the principal dancer with the Compaigne de Danse et Musique Hindou. His life changed after meeting Allaudin Khan, a famed multi-instrumentalist (and father of Ali Akbar Khan) in 1934 and becoming his apprentice. He abandoned dance in 1938 to devote himself to study of the sitar. Six years later he began to emerge, touring, composing for films—his "Sare Jahan Se Accha" was a hugely popular song of the period—and appearing on Indian Radio (he'd be their music director for seven years). Lauded at home as a master on the sitar, Shankar began touring internationally in the mid-1950s, with a reputation that was soon global, even if the audiences outside India tended to be small. That would, of course, change in the 1960s, when George Harrison of the Beatles began taking sitar lessons from Shankar, transforming the man into a star who could captivate audiences at both concert halls and pop festivals (he performed at Woodstock and at Monterey). In 1970 he became the first Indian composer to have a work commissioned by a Western orchestra, and he performed his "Concerto for Sitar and Orchestra" with the London Philharmonic. Since then he's written many pieces for Western ensembles. While his Indian reputation was built as a classical and popular musician and writer, since 1975 he's concentrated solely on Hindustani classical music, founding the Kinnara School of Music in Mumbai. In recent years he's made his home in California, where he's established the Ravi Shankar Foundation and served as the chair of the department of Indian music at the California Institute of the Arts. Now in his eighties, Shankar does still occasionally tour, although he seems to have largely passed the traditional musical torch to his daughter, Anoushka. Norah Jones, his other daughter, has been making waves in the jazz field.

Europe

Vera Bilá (b. 1954): Vera Bilá began singing as a child, although her parents tried to stop her. They understood that no Romany singer was going to be successful, particularly one from Rokycany in rural eastern Slovakia; that was simply the way of the world. But she persisted, even as she took a succession of low-paying jobs to pay the rent. She sang at weddings and dances, anywhere she could, eventually joining forces with the musicians who became the foundation of her group, Kale (Bilá means white, and Kale means black, hence Vera White and the Blacks). However, success still eluded them until Czech pop singer Zuzana Navarová offered them an opening slot at her Prague concert. From there they found a regular gig at a bar in town, with their heady mix of Brazilian rhythms behind Bilá's deep, expressive voice. They made their first album in 1995, which brought European attention. The follow-up, three years later, was released in America, bringing Bilá a whole new audience. She's become a symbol to the Romany people and a Czech icon: there was even a documentary about her, *Cerna a bila v barve* (Black and White in Color), in 1999. At three hundred fifty pounds and a little over five feet tall, she's an imposing figure and utterly charismatic once she opens her mouth to sing.

Martin Carthy, M.B.E. (b. 1940): Music wasn't Martin Carthy's initial love; the Briton initially gravitated toward the stage. It wasn't until he was nineteen that he made his debut on guitar, as the folk revival was beginning. A quick learner and an assiduous scholar of English folk music, he quickly made his mark on the fledgling 1960s London scene, teaching the traditional "Scarborough Fair" to a visiting Paul Simon, who'd use it with Simon and Garfunkel. His recorded solo debut came in 1965, since which time he's continued to make his own records, played with Steeleye Span, helped form the adventurous Brass Monkey, been a long-standing member of a cappella quartet the Watersons (he's married to Norma Waterson), kept a duo going with fiddler Dave Swarbrick, and been a major part of the family band Waterson: Carthy—among many other ventures. His interpretations of traditional music, especially the big ballads, have been luminous, while his highly idiosyncratic guitar technique (which tends to be spare and rhythmic) is masterful. His influence on at least two generations of folk performers, both in Britain and elsewhere, has been incalculable. He not only kept the folk revival alive after the initial push of the 1960s but expanded its reach. Carthy was awarded the Member of the British Empire for his services to folk music.

Manu Chao (b. 1961): Born Oscar Tramor in France, Manu Chao has become the impish prankster of modern world music. Inspired by the English punk he heard as a teenager, he eventually formed the band Mano Negra (named for a Spanish anarchist organization). They created a free, fluid fusion of punk, hip-hop, reggae, and Latin music, with lyrics in French, Spanish, and English—about as cross-cultural as it was possible to get. The band, which was one of the inspirations for the Latin alternative and Rock en Español movements, lasted until 1994, breaking up during a rail tour around South America. After that, Chao traveled, carrying portable recording equipment and putting down tracks when, where, and how he felt. The result was the basis for his first solo album, *Clandestino*, in 1998. It stripped away the confrontational edge of Mano Negra, leaving a playful, adventurous spirit who seemed to regard all of world music (especially the Latin side) as his canvas. He repeated the exercise, with more commercial success, on his second record. While capable of filling large venues in many parts of the world, he can often be found playing solo on the streets of Barcelona, where he makes his home.

The Chieftains (formed 1963): Probably no band in any style has played with as many guests as Ireland's Chieftains during their illustrious career. But they still line up to play with the group that's become a watchword for Celtic music and has done more to popularize it around the world than anyone else. Several of the musicians who make up the Chieftains were originally brought together by composer Seán Ó'Riada for his Ceoltoiri Chualann project, which changed the face of Irish music by creating an ensemble, rather than solo or duo instruments. Some of the players formed a side group, the Chieftains, and made what was intended to be a one-off debut in 1963. Both groups coexisted for much of the 1960s, before the Chieftains took on a life of their own. They were the unlikeliest stars—conservative, middle-aged men playing traditional Irish music with no gimmicks. They didn't even become full-time professional musicians until 1975. Since that time, under the leadership of whistle and uillean pipe master Paddy Moloney, they've maintained a feverish pace of touring and recording, including a number of movie soundtracks and a groundbreaking tour of China in 1983, where they invited local musicians to take the stage alongside them. They've explored the Celtic connections between Irish, Breton, and Galician music and delved into the Irish influence of American roots music. And though they attract more than their share of big musical names (Rolling Stones, Sting, and so on) to perform on their albums, the Chieftains are a band with the most thorough musical grounding, all virtuosos on their instruments. Unfortunately, harpist Derek Ball died in

2002. Although they record very little traditional Irish music these days, it remains the soul of their work.

The Gipsy Kings (formed 1979): The brand name in pop-flamenco, the Gipsy Kings began their career in southern France as Los Reyes, playing traditional flamenco music. After meeting producer Claude Martinez in 1986, they changed their sound, bringing in influences from the Middle East, rock, and Latin music. It proved to be an astute move; the following year, two of their singles made the French charts. Their eponymous album was a hit in many European countries, and on its U.S. release, spent a stunning forty weeks on the American charts. Since then they've softened their sound a little, making it accessible to an even wider audience. Popularity might have come at the expense of real authenticity, but a real flamenco heart still beats under all the trappings.

Boris Grebenshikov (b. 1953): Born in Leningrad, Russia, Boris Grebenshikov loved Western rock in his youth and would translate the lyrics of the songs he heard on Western radio into Russian to perform them with his own band. In the 1970s, he formed Aquarium, which ran afoul of the government when they refused to submit their songs to the censorship committees. Without state sanction, their only way to be heard was through the underground network of venues, and that was how they survived until perestroika turned things upside down in the mid-1980s and their sound became acceptable. Grebenshikov began a parallel solo career in 1984, bringing Russian folk traditions into his songs. In 1989 he recorded a solo album in the West, but still makes his home in Russia.

Paco de Lucia (b. 1947): The greatest flamenco guitarist of modern times has also been one of the most innovative. Spain's

Paco de Lucia has nipped and bitten at the edges of the form, bringing in jazz, Brazilian, and North African music. He began playing at the age of five, made his performing debut at the age of eleven, and his recording debut at age fourteen. Two years later he was touring internationally with a flamenco dance troupe. His first solo album (he'd already made several records with others) came in 1967, the year before he began working with the eminent singer El Camarón de la Isla. The ten discs they made together stand as a high water mark of the flamenco art. With a highly developed technique and a master's ear for the right note in the right place, de Lucia quickly became *the* flamenco guitarist, in touch with the soul of the music. That was fine, but it wasn't enough. The 1970s found him branching out, making jazz records with Al DiMeola, John McLaughlin, and others and finding favor with fans outside Spain. For a while, at the beginning of the 1980s, he fronted a nueva flamenco sextet, including electric instruments, before pulling back to a more sedate acoustic trio. The 1990s saw him flirt with jazz once more, along with classical music and Arabic music, and then return, finally, to the passion of flamenco.

Amália Rodrigues (1920–1999): Amália Rodrigues was the undisputed queen of fado, a woman whose voice was pure emotion. Born in the Alfama district of Portugal's capital, Lisbon, the home of fado, she was one of ten children raised by her grandmother after her mother abandoned them. Although she made her initial performance at the age of nine, it wasn't until she was fifteen that her singing career really began. Her big break would come in 1940, when she took part in the revue *Ora Vai Tu!* (Listen You Go!) at Lisbon's Maria Vitório Theater. She became an instant star in Lisbon, filling clubs all over the city, even during wartime. Three years later, she began making appearances in Spain and Brazil before she embarked on a successful film career. However, although she was already a big star and a huge concert draw, she didn't make her first record until 1951—her manager believed that if people could hear her on disc, they wouldn't pay to see her live. But the reverse was true; her popularity soared, and she undertook a world tour, which saw her headline in New York without even having released a record in the United States. Although the popularity of fado diminished during the 1960s, she was already a national icon. She released more than 170 albums during a career that spanned fifty years, finally retiring in the 1990s, after which she was celebrated by a week-long documentary series on Portuguese television, *Amália—Uma Estranha Forma de Vida*. Following her death in 1999, there was a day of mourning throughout Portugal, and her remains were enshrined in the National Pantheon.

Värttinä (formed 1983): Värttinä began in 1983 as a twenty-one-strong group of young girls in Finland's Karelia area who'd gather together to recite the old poems and sing the traditional songs. Until 1989, they were all quite happy doing that. But at that point, when they were dispersing for college and the band appeared likely to end, founder Sari Kaasinen brought in new members, and the "real" Värttinä was born. Still led by female singers and performing traditional music (with a decidedly feminist slant in the lyrics), they quickly found success, with a top-ten single and big-selling album. They capitalized on that, without ever compromising the music or the sound, to jump to a world stage as their albums gained international release and acclaim. With an excellent band of musicians behind them, the women sang in the loud, keening Karelian style that's still their trademark. Since 1998 they've reached full maturity (with some personnel changes, including the departure of leader Kaasinen), making more complex music and adding their own songs, heavily influenced by traditional Finno-Ugric and runo-song, into the mix.

The Americas

Susana Baca (b.?): Growing up surrounded by music in the Peruvian coastal town of Chorrillos, the one thing Susana Baca didn't hear was the music that described her—Afro-Peruvian. The only place it was available was at home, and she absorbed it by osmosis. In many ways, Afro-Peruvians hardly existed. Baca's mission was to change that. In addition to singing, she began researching her own culture and its music. Seven years later, helped by her husband, she produced *Del Fuego y del Agua*, a historical document (book and CD) that traced Afro-Peruvian history. That spurred Baca to start Instituto Negro Continuo in 1992, intended to promote the awareness and acceptance of Afro-Peruvian culture. Although she was a singer, she was more known for her folklore work. That changed in 1995, when she appeared on the compilation *The Sound of Black Peru*, singing "Maria Lando," and her sultry, silky voice created a minor sensation. Her eponymous debut arrived in 1997 and delivered everything people hoped for; she was backed simply by guitar and cajón, or rhythm box. From that minimalist start, her music has become more complex, but never crowded, while her sense of adventure keeps increasing.

Alan Lomax (1915–2002): If not for American Alan Lomax, the world might never have heard Leadbelly, Muddy Waters, or literally hundreds of other artists. Lomax might not have made music himself, but as a musicologist he recorded those who did. Son of another celebrated musicologist, John Lomax, he first hit the road in the 1930s, helping his father gather material for the Library of Congress' Archive of American Folksong in the southern states. On that trip, they recorded Leadbelly for the first time. Nine years later, in Mississippi, Lomax would record a young McKinley Morganfield, who'd become better known as Muddy Waters. While best known for the music he collected in the United States, Lomax was a global traveler, with a hunger for music and the knack of eliciting some wonderful performances. He worked extensively in the Caribbean, and for much of the 1950s made his home in England, using that as a base while recording throughout the British Isles and Ireland. His fieldwork in Spain and Italy, where little had been done before, was especially influential— in fact, his recordings in Italy were the first survey of the country's music. In 1959 he returned to the United States to live and work, and on a trip south unearthed Mississippi Fred McDowell, who hadn't recorded since the 1920s. An academic, he formulated his theory of Cantometrics in the 1960s for evaluating song performances. During the 1970s and 1980s he broadcast the *American Patchwork* television series and wrote *The Land Where the Blues Began* before beginning work on the Global Jukebox, a multimedia project designed to tie together all the strands of his work. In the late 1990s, a comprehensive series of reissues of Lomax's work began.

Los Tigres del Norte (formed 1968): Although Mexican Americans Los Tigres del Norte live in San Jose and have won a Grammy, their profile among Anglos in the United States is minimal. To Mexicans and Mexican Americans, though, they're icons. In 1968, three Hernández brothers, musicians from the village of Rosa Morada, along with their cousin, were hired to play a Mexican Independence Day celebration in San Jose, California. The only problem was that the oldest of them was just fourteen. However, he'd been playing professionally since he was eight. The group crossed the border with help, but not before the U.S. Customs had called them "tigers," a name that stuck. The group played their norteño music for the crowd, then added another show—and never went home. They signed with the local Fama label and began playing electric instruments, something new for the style. Their initial breakthrough came in 1972, with the corrido "Contrabando y Traición." It was, really, the first of the violent narcocorridos, fueling a boom that's still going. Within four years, they'd begun expanding their range to chronicle the Mexican immigrant experience, something they knew at firsthand. Since then, they've recorded both narcocorridos and very political immigrant songs, both of which have made them hugely popular with the Mexican population they address. A 1987 Grammy and a 2000 Latin Grammy did acknowledge their status as Mexico's premier norteño band. Their albums remain consistent best-sellers within the Mexican community, and their shows sell out quickly. They've also given back to their people, among other things establishing a multimillion-dollar scholarship at the University of California at Los Angeles.

Bob Marley (1945–1981): Without doubt, Jamaica's Bob Marley remains the best-known name in reggae. The image of him onstage, holding a guitar, dreadlocks swinging, is one of the music's most enduring. The son of an Englishman and a Jamaican, he came of age in Kingston's Trenchtown ghetto. With his friends Peter McIntosh and Neville Livingstone (who would become Peter Tosh and Bunny Wailer), he formed the Wailers, a singing trio. Their first hit came in 1963 with the classic "Simmer Down." Over the next three years the hits kept on coming, with Marley developing as a songwriter. In 1966, Marley moved to the United States, working at a Chrysler plant in Delaware for several months before returning to Jamaica. The Wailers resumed recording, releasing material on their own label. Toward the end of the decade they began working with producer Lee Perry and his house band, the Upsetters (some of whom would join the Wailers). It was a fruitful incubation period that saw the band develop by leaps and bounds. Many of Marley's best songs were written during this time, like "Small Axe" and "400 Years," while Perry worked with them on developing a solid style, experimenting with new ideas. On a promise of a record deal, the Wailers moved to London, only to have their hopes dashed—until they met Chris Blackwell, head of Island Records. He financed a recording, although when Marley brought him the tapes, Blackwell insisted on remixing them and adding some lead guitar and keyboards to make the music palatable to a white rock audience. It worked. The album sold reasonably, if not remarkably. It was certainly eclipsed by the follow-up, *Burnin'*, which contained "I Shot the Sheriff," made into a major rock hit by Eric Clapton. His version might have been bland, but it introduced reggae to a whole new audience and helped make big stars of the Wailers. However, the trio was fracturing, and by the time of the next record, *Natty Dread*, which included the anthemic "No Woman No Cry," Tosh and Wailer had departed. Marley stepped into the limelight well, proving to be a charismatic frontman and consolidating his position—and his music—with 1975's *Live!*. The following year he survived an assassination attempt the night before he was to perform at a concert aimed to bring peace to the Jamaican general election. He performed, then left the country for almost two years, during which time he released some of his most potent work on *Exodus* and *Survival*. His songs grew more political, and he began looking more closely at Africa—where he toured in 1980, cementing his legendary status on the continent. He died of cancer in 1981 and was buried in the Jamaican countryside. But his reputation has continued to grow. Many of the songs he wrote have become reggae classics, and his influence as an artist is still very obvious in the reggae coming out of Africa and Latin America.

Beny Moré (1919–1963): Dubbed "El Bárbarao Del Ritmo" (The Barbarian of Rhythm), Beny Moré is probably the single most influential singer to have come out of Cuba. However, he was equally talented as a musician and arranger, making him a powerhouse of Cuban music. Born Bartolome Maximilliano Moré Guiterrez in Santa Isabel de las Lajas, he started out by playing guitar at dances and festivals, but by the time he was twenty, he was in Havana and starting to make his name as a singer. In 1945 he toured Mexico with Conjunto Matamoras and ended up staying in the country a little while, eventually working with the great Perez Prado. They were a powerful combination, and fame quickly followed as they helped revolutionize Latin music with the mambo. By 1953, Moré was ready to go home. Back in Cuba he formed Orquesta Gigante, which backed him on the greatest records of his career, ones that were profoundly important in the development of the Cuban sound. He died at the age of forty-three, in large part due to his offstage excesses.

R. Carlos Nakai (b. 1946): Navajo-Ute Carlos Nakai has gained fame as a Native American flutist who's crossed boundaries from traditional to New Age and classical music. He wanted to play flute as a boy but was pushed toward trumpet by a teacher, which he played until 1970, when he smashed his lip in an accident. He began playing flute in 1982 and started researching traditional Native American music, producing his first recording the following year. Although he's found success with "outer culture," the heart of his music has remained Native American, and he was the first artist to receive a gold record for Native music, for 1989's *Canyon Trilogy*. In the years since, he's become almost a brand name, renowned for his haunting flute work. His curiosity has taken him into New Age, jazz, and even some world music. In the new millennium he became more ambitious, attempting music that was virtually symphonic in scope.

Astor Piazzolla (1921–1992): When Piazzolla began his experiments with the tango, his fellow Argentinians derided him as the assassin of the tango. Combining the national dance and its sultry, steamy melodies and rhythm with jazz and classical music was sacrilege. But he persisted and transformed it into nuevo tango, a music for listening rather than dancing. Piazzolla was in some ways a hybrid himself. His parents moved to New York when he was three, and he grew up in Little Italy, starting lessons on bandoneon almost from the time he could hold one. Fascinated by jazz, he was taken by the music of Duke Ellington. After the family returned to Argentina, he began classical training, then joined a tango orchestra. He vacillated between classical and tango music for a number of years before dedicating himself solely to tango. Finally he achieved some acceptance for his ideas in the 1980s, with *Tango: Zero Hour* offering an international manifesto for his ideas, which received a wider airing in the Broadway hit *Tango Argentina*. His final performance came in 1990.

Tito Puente (1923–2000): For fully half a century, America's Tito Puente was the face of Latin music in the United States. A superb player of timbales and other percussion instruments, he was also a gifted arranger and composer and a consummate showman. With Puerto Rican parents, he was raised in New York's Spanish Harlem and hoped to become a dancer, until a childhood ankle injury made that impossible. Instead, he started drumming professionally when he was thirteen, before attending Juilliard. Following World War II, he played with Latin pioneer Machito and then formed his own band, the Picadilly Boys. Throughout the 1950s he worked tirelessly for Latin music, helping popularize the mambo and the cha-cha-cha. He recorded numerous albums, and his incendiary live shows became legendary, earning him the title El Rey, "The King." He not only performed Latin music but also gave the Latin treatment to jazz standards and show tunes, employing a number of musicians who went on to fame in their own right, from Johnny Pacheco to Doc Severinesen. The winner of many Grammy awards (his first came in 1983), he maintained a rigorous touring schedule throughout his life and rode the Latin boom of the 1950s and the salsa fad of the 1970s, before gaining the respect of the jazz world for his later, sophisticated Latin jazz. Outside Latin circles, he's probably most familiar as the composer of "Oye Como Va," which was a 1960s hit for Santana. Releasing more than a hundred albums during his lifetime, he was a groundbreaker in the acceptance of Latin music in the United States.

Caetano Veloso (b. 1942): Caetano Veloso has become one of Brazil's most revered musicians, but his first love was cinema; he ended up in music more or less by accident, thanks to the influence of bossa nova star João Gilberto. Born in Bahia in northern Brazil, he followed his sister, singer Maria Bethânia, to Rio de Janeiro, where he began winning songwriting contests, eventually recording his own album. Meeting another northerner, Gilberto Gil, proved to be a turning point. Together, they were the heart of the new tropicália movement, which imported ideas from rock with poetic lyrics and electric instruments. Their revolutionary ideas fell foul of the dictatorship government, and they were forced into exile in England. When they returned, they found many of their ideas had gradually found their way into the mainstream, and Veloso was a star. Curiously, he didn't appear in North America until 1983, and none of his albums was available in the United States until 1987. Since that time each new disc and tour has cemented his status as a cultural ambassador for Brazil and a powerful songwriter and performer in his own right. But he continues to look ahead and experiment with his music, refusing to stand still.

FIVE

The Music

N o songs "typify" world music; nothing represents the whole world. And the pieces listed here don't claim to be representative, by any means. But each one offers something special, whether from the artist or from the style. All are exceptional performances and often groundbreaking in their own way. They might not be the best work the artist has ever done, but they catch something important from their oeuvre.

Many of these were recorded within the past twenty years. That's relatively recent, but much recorded world music is from the past two decades, and it doesn't diminish their significance. Obviously, not every area of world music is included in this chapter; that's simply not possible. But in this list are many of the vital strands of world music.

Africa and the Middle East

"365 Is My Number/The Message" (King Sunny Adé and His African Beats, 1982): Adé had long been a star in his native Nigeria when Island Records tried to promote him to international fame in 1982 with *JuJu Music*. Taken from that album, this track shows just how he'd made juju into *his* music. Adé sings in English, but in many respects the vocals hardly matter; they stand more as breaks and bookmarks between the instrumental workouts and the call-and-response between instruments and talking drums that characterize Adé's sound. His innovation of adding pedal steel guitar is startling, but effective and surprisingly natural (the same, unfortunately, can't be said for the synthesizers on the track). Multilayered percussion bubbles underneath, as three guitars and the steel interlock ideas and spiky, rhythmic riffs. Martin Meisonnier's modern production, with lots of echo and touches of dub, actually works against the music, when he could have simply boosted the bass and the drums. But the power and flow remains undeniable, with the talking drums still speaking more loudly than any vocalist. At just over eight minutes, it's short by real Adé workout standards—in concert it's not unusual for songs to last twenty minutes or more—but it gives more than a hint as to his hypnotic power. Listen particularly for the talking drum interjections and comments on the action, both vocal and musical.

"Gannit Naimi" (Oum Kalsoum, 1932): Also known as Um Kulthum, or Oum Kalthoum, the Mother of the Arabs, as she was nicknamed, was perhaps the greatest Arab singer of modern times. This composition, with the music by Daoud Hosni and words from poet Ahmed Rami (who'd taught Kalsoum a great deal about literature after she moved to Cairo), exemplifies her stunning articulation and way of ornamenting a line. Working with a small, oud-led ensemble, her melismatic voice carries the complex song with its aching, mournful melody. Her relatively dry vibrato is stunning, as is the deep wellspring of emotion she can readily command. Mostly, however, it's notable for the sheer authority of her singing. Her timing is impeccable, as is her sense of tone throughout. There's a charisma that extends beyond the song, and even beyond the limitations of recording at the time. And there's also an intimacy in her style that makes it very personal, even if you don't understand the lyrics. It's easy to feel as if she were singing just to you, and you alone. Utterly hypnotic, she absorbed the classical past of Arab music and remade it as something new.

"Immigrés" (Youssou N'Dour and Super Etoile de Dakar, 1984): Youssou N'Dour's song to those Senegalese working abroad, reminding them not to forget their homeland, was his European breakthrough, and for many the first taste of his mbalax. With the stuttering sabar, or talking drum, cutting across the beat, and Jimmy Mbaye's spiky lead guitar adding the flavor of Africanized rock, this is a complete group effort, down to the horn punctuations. But it's N'Dour's voice that mesmerizes, arriving in an impossibly high griot wail that demands attention, then caressing the lines. At the time, it was unlike anything else to have come out of West Africa, a powerhouse of rhythm that didn't quit. It was the first full flowering of N'Dour's style, with startling tempo shifts that never lost the melody. Not the best mbalax he'd ever record, it does highlight the fluidity and flexibility of his voice, while showcasing all the other elements he was bringing into his music and breaking with the Cuban music he'd sung in the past. This is the point at which it all became completely Senegalese, a real breakthrough that heralded something fresh and new. But neither N'Dour nor the band ever sound tentative about these new steps; instead, they steam into it, with hearts on their sleeves.

"Ngicabange Ngaqeda" (Mahlathini Nezintombi Zomgoashiyo, 1986): From the seminal compilation, *The Indestructible Beat of Soweto*, this was the first time most of the world heard Mahlathini, the "Groaner," with his deep, lion-like bass voice. With the wonderfully electrified mbaqanga rhythm behind him, provided by the Makgona Tshole Band, and the Zulu harmonies of the female backing (the Mahotella Queens, with whom he recorded for years), this is the true sound of the South African townships. They continue the Mbube vocal tradition, a conversation between female and male, while the guitar offers some stunning, countrified lead playing when not pushing the rhythm, and the melodic elastic bass style, so typical of mbaqanga, grabs the ear every bit as much as the voices. Together, voices and music exert an almost irresistible pull to dance, showing that some of the most glorious music can be made in the harshest conditions. The song (the title means "I Have Made Up My Mind") is actually about female strength, a woman complaining to her parents about her man, who insults her when he's drunk, and her parents saying, "Let him go, he is not a man / He is a drunkard!" Recorded in the early 1980s, this is a perfect example of the urban pop style that had been popular in black South Africa for a number of years.

"On Entre O.K., On Sort K.O." (Franco, 1956): The title translates as "You come in O.K., you leave knocked out," the signature tune of guitar wizard Franco and his band O.K. Jazz. It's pure self-aggrandizement, but more than justified. The band had barely existed for a year when they recorded this song, an ideal early example of Congolese rumba. Because of recording limitations of the period, it doesn't bring in the extended sebene, or instrumental section, that would characterize much of the group's later work, but instead it's a short, three-minute punch. The rumba elements are already in place, with multiple vocalists, a strong but unobtrusive rhythm section, and the three guitars—rhythm, semilead, and lead, with Franco at the forefront—weaving short runs of majesty and magic, with a nagging riff surrounding the verses. This is music for dancing, and from the opening notes it's intended to move the feet. While it doesn't show much of Franco's genius on the fretboard, it's one of the seminal tracks of Congolese rumba, taking it from the early acoustic style of the late 1940s and plugging it in to the amplifiers. The pace is a little faster (though hardly the breakneck speed of soukous, which would develop from rumba), and it's impossible to hear this and not imagine couples on the dance floor.

"Sanougnaoule" (Kandia Kouyate, 2002): This piece is modern but it's a perfect distillation of the Malian djelimuso (or female griot) art. The song (whose title translates as "Face of Gold") is a praise song, in Maninka, detailing the worthy heritage of one Adam Souko and the noble antecedents of his wife—thus combining praise and the history for which djelimusos are known. Kouyate's regal voice is majestic throughout, stunning in its rough clarity, piercing at times, and soaring over the backing vocals. Her band isn't completely traditional, since she includes Latin percussion, among other things, in the lineup, but here it's down to some excellent basics, with African flute decorating the melody while the balafon (a kind of large wooden xylophone) gives the songs its main building blocks. The kora offers a rippling solo, and guest Djelimady Tounkara, the great musician from the Super Rail Band, also offers musical commentary (his stunning art is even more in evidence on "San Barana," another track on the same disc). But marvelous as the band sounds, they're all secondary to Kouyate herself. She dives between notes, holds them, then swoops across a difficult line with grace and certainty. Kouyate has been acknowledged as the greatest living djelimuso, and on the basis of this track, it's easy to understand why; she's easily the equal of any female singer, anywhere in the world.

"Shuffering and Shmiling" (Fela Anikulapo Kuti, 1977): Fela Kuti was nothing if not confrontational, and this attack on the cultural imperialism of non-African religions is a prime example of his art. In part it's an attack on Nigeria's Christian president, and also on a Muslim businessman who was one of Kuti's enemies, but it's also a comment on the violence in Nigeria between Christians and Muslim fundamentalists. Musically, it's an excellent example of Kuti's Afrobeat, where interlocking short, funky riffs create a foundation over the energetic but subtle drumming, allowing for lengthy solos on the top (such as the trumpet and saxophone here). This track actually made up an entire album in Nigeria, the music enjoying a lengthy exposition and development—some nine and a half minutes—before Kuti enters as a vocalist, singing in pidgin English. The band is like clockwork behind him, perfectly drilled but with a loose, supple feel, while he slides out his militant words. By this time he'd perfected the balance between American soul and funk and Nigerian highlife polyrhythms; and the ease with which the group follows him, even through his strange scatting, is testament to how well the form worked, with its repeated tensions and releases. The essence of think and dance, Kuti proved that politics and music could mix.

Asia

"Aloha 'Oe" (Ozzie Kotani, 2002): Probably the most famous and immediately recognizable Hawaiian song, "Aloha 'Oe" was composed by Queen Lilu'uokalani (1838–1917) in the 1870s (borrowing from a couple of American parlor songs). After the Royal Hawaiian Band began playing it in the United States in the 1880s, it became globally known. This version, played on solo slack-key guitar in a drop C tuning, makes a few melodic changes to the verses, but leaves the famous chorus intact. With a new introduction and coda and a subtle change in the verse chording, the song is stripped of both its luau connotations and its vocals to reveal a piece of very delicate beauty that solo guitar brings out brilliantly. This version never denies the lulling, wave-like rhythm that's part of the song's appeal, but neither does it emphasize it; instead, Kotani focuses on the melody, allowing it to breathe and resolving it masterfully into the chorus. Queen Lili'oukalani was a prolific composer, with a strong sense of Hawaiian tradition, but she was also well aware of modern musical trends and often managed to marry the two—but rarely better than on "Aloha 'Oe." To hear it presented this way, though, is nothing short of a revelation that lets you forget all the kitsch trappings generally associated with the piece, and to hear, almost for the first time, its very pure beauty.

"Deke-Jo" (Huun-Huur-Tu, 1999): Tuvan throat singing exists in five styles, and this piece illustrates three of them—kargyraa, sygyt, and xöömei. Kargyraa is the most dynamic, with its subharmonics generally an octave below the note actually being sung. Sygyt is a two-note style, and xöömei can be both a three-note style and a word used to collectively describe the entire range of throat singing. Over the rhythm of a cantering horse (endemic to Tuvan music, where horses remain a vital part of life) provided by bull testicles, Huun-Huur-Tu provide a mix of folk singing, throat singing, and instruments. The kargyraa is the most spectacular—shadowing the words on the second verse, while the higher xöömei, almost like a whistle, closes the brief piece. But in less than two and a half minutes, the band offers a near-perfect distillation of Tuvan styles. The doshpuluur, a three-string instrument reminiscent of a banjo, provides the instrumental melody, but it's the vocals that are arresting. The throat singing here isn't just tonal, it's true singing of words and lines, which is especially artful and remarkable, and quite spectacular. The technique can be learned, although it can damage the throat if not done properly. But this is a quartet of masters. Something that's often overlooked, because of that ability, is the fact that they're also excellent instrumentalists, too, with a deep knowledge of their folk traditions; throat singing is only one of their talents, although it's the most obvious (especially for Kaigal-ool Khovalyg).

"Máru Bihág" (Ravi Shankar, 1968): This evening raga, with its strong feminine quality of longing, offers a melancholy beauty. Working around an ascending and descending line in a major scale, it still curiously produces a minor mood. The tala, or rhythm, is ten-beat matra, stated by Chatur Lal on tablas, while N. C. Mullick provides instrumental support on tambura. Shankar's sitar playing is cleanly immaculate and understatedly emotive throughout. He keeps the structure shimmering, allowing himself freedom on the opening alaap, which sets the mood, and offers imaginative improvisation throughout, embellishing the mood of the raga in the jor section before showing his skill and speed of thought on the more rapid jhala, where his fingers move with rapid grace. To hear Shankar play the sitar is to move into another world, where the complexities of Indian classical music seem obvious and simple. There's a great fluidity in his playing, and his phrases carry through the rhythm, moving over it, rather than just within it. It's the sound of an inspired master at work, and it becomes easy to hear why George Harrison was so struck by his playing.

"Mustt Mustt" (Lost in His Work) (Nusrat Fateh Ali Khan, 1990): When there's so much excellent work by Nusrat working within his Sufi tradition, accompanied by his own "party," it seems churlish to select this more adventurous track on which all but one of the musicians accompanying the Pakistani legend is Western. But the funky backing proves to be a brilliant foil for his improvisational qualities, which rapidly take wing, soaring through the stratosphere. One of the great extemporizers, he shows in this piece how he could work a note or a phrase, throwing it around, then meditating on it. His music was meant to be an ecstatic, religious experience, and that's what this becomes. The musicians keep themselves in the background, allowing the voice to shine, going higher and higher through the track, as the music seems to possess him. At five minutes, this is very short by Nusrat's standards, but there's beauty in its brevity, and the rhythmically familiar, electric backing forms an easy way to enter the world of qawwali, while still hearing some of the best of Nusrat, who, particularly toward the end, simply shimmers in his incandescent vocal.

"So Gaye Hain" (A. R. Rahman, 2000): Composed for the movie *Zubeidaa*, this is a prime illustration of Rahman's use of melodies. Delicately voiced by Lata Mangeshkar, it follows a Western song structure of verses and bridge, letting melodies build on top of each other, with subtly dramatic orchestration. Apart from the accent and language of the singer, it would be almost impossible to pick this out as Indian, especially from the arrangement and the swirling strings that herald the final verse. Instantly memorable, and slightly exotic while being gorgeously romantic—though never over the top, even when the choir enters—it's the culmination of what Rahman's learned in his brief, but very successful, Bollywood career. He's not afraid to pile on the melodies, almost to the point of overload, but always stopping at just the right point. This is the sophisticated end of Indian movie music that's learned from the West but is confident enough to assert its own ideas. Rahman innately understands how to get the best from the range of an orchestra, how to use it both dramatically and lyrically, in a way that brings both a sweep of sound and intimacy.

Europe

"A La Turk" (Taraf de Haïdouks, 2001): The entire sense of Balkan Romany music crammed into six minutes of extraordinary music. Recorded live, Romania's Taraf de Haïdouks are accompanied by clarinetist Filip Simeonov and the Koçani Orkestar Gypsy Brass Band. After a virtuosic clarinet intro, everyone takes off full-tilt into the piece, playing at hair-raising speed in compound time—analogous to speeding down a winding mountain road without any brakes. When you think they can't go any faster, the violin, accordion, and cimballon (a kind of hammer dulcimer) simply speed up. This is true Balkan village music, albeit at a very high skill level. Fiddler Neculae Neacsu (now deceased, and then in his late seventies), plays with incredible style, coaxing impossible notes and phrases from his instrument. The fact that this is meant to be grandiose showboating becomes irrelevant: it's heart-stoppingly exciting, and once the brass kicks in, wildly extravagant, with percussion punctuations from the darbuka that send the temperature even higher. It's the ideal piece for becoming a convert to both Balkan and Gypsy music: furious, fiery, and completely addictive.

"Kyla Vuotti Uutta Kuuta" (Värttinä, 1992): This traditional song gave Värttinä their only chart hit in their native Finland. Actually a Karelian wedding song, sung by the groom's sister to welcome the bride to her new home, it's slower and more lyrical than much of their repertoire of the period. The harmonies of the four singers is typically Karelian, with a piercing quality that's even more evident in the solo passages. The fiddle breaks echo the vocal melody, and organ chords underpin the singing, unusual for this band, which has generally used accordion. At this stage, Värttinä was still investigating traditional music rather than delving into the runo-song and original material that would later become their trademark. The beauty of the piece is in its simple elegance, and several members of the twelve-member group advisedly sit out on this rather than cluttering the arrangement. It's educational to compare this with a live version recorded eight years later, when most of the lineup had changed. On the newer one, bouzouki and guitar provide much of the backing, offering a more Celtic feel, and the harmonies are smoother (as is the solo singing), and Kari Reiman's violin decorates the melody more. It's still beautiful, but lacking the simple grace that makes the 1992 take so remarkable.

"Señor Calice" (Lo'Jo, 1999): This cut manages to explore much of the music of new multicultural France within the first minute. Denis Péan's gruff vocal conjures up Serge Gains-bourg, the accordion offers images of sidewalk cafés and bal musette, while the violin brings in fiery Gypsy tones. And then the harmonies of the Nid El Mourid sisters introduce the Algerians, the *beurs* who've grown up in France—all over a spiky, jazzy rhythm. To top it off, the Gangbé Brass Band, from Benin, offer wild horns and a rap that briefly turns the song in an entirely different direction. Add to that the fact that the song's in Spanish, with a rich underpinning of lay-ered percussion, and there's something that's perhaps as rep-resentative of France today as any song can be. The vocal melody has obvious roots in chanson, but composer Péan uses that as nothing more than a springboard, bringing in the ele-ments that surround him in everyday life, the cultures that feed into the stream or modern-day France. The way the ele-ments balance could be seen as an allegory of the country—or simply the skill of the band, who've created something unique out of the materials they've found.

"The Claudy Banks" (Bob and Jim Copper, 1951): One of the most popular "broken-token" songs, dating from the early nine-teenth century, this has been collected numerous times across Britain, Ireland, the United States, and Australia. The Coppers, part of the illustrious English folk-singing Copper Family, recorded this version for the BBC. The two voices offer an interesting mix of trading off lines and har-monies. Typical of English music, there's very little decora-tion of the melody in the presentation (e.g., as one might find in Irish singing); it's straightforward, with just enough variation to maintain interest and keep the drama of the song, which is happily resolved in the final verse. By offer-ing a very plain version of "The Claudy Banks" (a song that has become a folk staple), the singers emphasize the story, rather than the singing, a trait of southern English singers that might well stem from the plain hymn singing of the Church of England.

"The Well below the Valley" (Planxty, 1973): Collected from John Reilly of County Roscommon, other versions of this traditional song appear as Child's Ballad No. 21. Based on the story of Jesus at the well, many older singers refused to perform it because of its dark overtones. But Planxty illuminate it, the bodhran and mandolin cushioning the voices on the insistent chorus, while Liam O'Flynn's uillean pipes offer an underpinning drone. Planxty don't try to explain the mystical, allegorical tale, but their performance is magical, the whistles and pipe forming an eerie coda to the song. With its sense of foreboding, it's the antithesis of the popular, lively image of Irish music, and it doesn't contain the melodic grace of the loveliest airs. It seems to reach back further, with its very basic structure of repetitive chorus, to become something more primal and more basically Irish. By keeping the instrumentation at a minimum, just enough for texture and coloring, the band keeps the focus firmly on the voices, while the ragged harmony on the chorus simply drives it home. It's a powerful song that demands a powerful rendition, which is what it receives here, charismatic in its simplicity.

"Yo, Marinero" (Diego Carrasco, 2000): The international image of Spanish flamenco has become tainted over the years. The guitar is a vital instrument, but flamenco is also a very vocal music. Carrasco, from Jerez, understands that perfectly well. This song strips away all the gloss that's surrounded the music. The handclaps (palmas) endemic to flamenco provide the rhythm and create the atmosphere for Carrasco's gruff voice, which works closely with the guitar. The instrument improvises, offering comments and fleeting runs, but it's the voice that carries this. The emotion is palpable throughout, both in the singing and the silences, when only the palmas carry the song. It's not pure, traditional flamenco by any means, but it offers the same catharsis and duende as classic songs. And the roots of Carrasco's music are very firmly planted within the tradition, even as he carries it forward, which has won him the respect of purists, who can appreciate how he's working within the form, and of a new generation, who admire how he's advancing it. And this most definitely isn't the nueva flamenco, with its smooth edges and more obvious melodies. Carrasco can sometimes be ungainly in his singing, but the heartfelt power behind it outweighs any deficiencies.

The Americas

"Alegria, Alegria" (Caetano Veloso, 1967): Probably the single most famous song of Brazil's tropicália movement of the late 1960s, Veloso's aim was to marry Brazilian music with global influences—rock, folk, and pop. He succeeded to the extent that when he first performed the song he was roundly booed by those who wanted their Brazilian music to be nationalistic—and for the fact that he was backed by a rock band. It's not the best of his songs, callow, with the political lyrics self-consciously arty, and some of the psychedelia a little overstated, but it's surely one of the most significant, taking Brazil outside its own borders for the first time. Although the presentation is superficially like any mid-1960s rock song from the United Kingdom or United States, there's a lot more going on underneath, with a rhythm that's less than obvious and lyrics that are replete with allusions to the happenings within the country under the dictatorship. Even the title, which translates as "Joy, Joy," drips with irony. It's both an art statement and a manifesto for what the tropicálistas wanted to achieve. At that time and place, it demanded a reaction, be it positive or negative, and it received one, as Veloso was criticized by both the right and the left for his temerity. To his credit, he didn't let that deter him. In retrospect, it might be gauche, and very much of its time in sound and production, but it remains a vitally important song in the history of Brazilian popular music.

"Angelo" (Inti-Illimani, 1992): While the obvious influence here is the Andean tradition, with its high pipes (actually piccolo and flute substituting for panpipes), this heavily arranged piece also draws from other areas, such as the flamenco flourishes on guitar, while the deep cajon provides a rhythmic grounding. Essentially a simple lyrical melody, it's allowed to build intelligently and artfully, with a sense of release at the end of each chorus. The high strum of the charango keeps a strongly Andean feel throughout, while changes from major to minor key serve as reminders of the fact that Europe has also helped shape the flow and structure of all Latin music, and the rhythm shows small touches of the Africans who were brought as slaves. Also of note is the fact that the band recorded this in Chile, for the first time since they'd been forced into exile, making it into an important, celebratory homecoming.

"Chan Chan" (Buena Vista Social Club, 1997): Compay Segundo's country style son has rapidly achieved classic status. Although recent, it *feels* as if it had been around for decades. The lead vocal is handled excellently by Eliades Ochoa, who brings his years of experience in the more rural guajiro style to the song, while Segundo himself handles the deep harmony (Segundo, in fact, prefers to sing bass harmony) and the congas that gently push the song. While the slow, lulling structure is really all the song needs, it's also highlighted by a soft trumpet solo (far from the brashness usually associated with Cuban music) and Ochoa's own twinkling acoustic guitar. Producer Ry Cooder adds little atmospheric touches of electric guitar but keeps himself well in the background throughout. Even more than the performance, which is flawless, it's the song that's the standout, as fine an example of son as anyone is likely to find. Simple, but with logic and elegance, it's graceful. The Chan Chan and Juanika of the song made their first appearance in a song from the beginning of the twentieth century, before Segundo revived them. Since its appearance on this disc the song's been covered several times, most notably by Cuban hip-hop group Orishas, who presented it with a great deal of respect as "537-C.U.B.A" on their debut record.

"Contrabando Y Traición" (Los Tigres del Norte, 1972): This song, which the band heard in Los Angeles, represents the first step of the narcocorrido trend. The band members were all still in their teens when they recorded this, but they come at it with plenty of authority. The stripped-down sound, with the accordion as the lead instrument, is typical of 1970s norteño, albeit with a fiery edge that suits the lyric perfectly. The song, about a pair of smugglers bringing marijuana from Tijuana to California, culminates in a violent, fatal end, complete with the sound effects of guns being fired. It took several attempts for the band to cut it they way they wanted it to be—indeed, they almost gave up on it. Their persistence paid off in ways they couldn't imagine, catapulting them to superstardom in the Mexican and Mexican American communities, while the song itself spawned two sequels and three movies, and a whole new genre, which the band has returned to often over the years.

"Corcovado" (João Gilberto, 1960): Gilberto gave life to the compositions of Antonio Carlos Jobim. Jobim created bossa nova, which distilled the sound of samba through jazz, but Gilberto gave it living, breathing expression. This track is an ideal example of bossa's possibilities. Gilberto's underrated guitar playing subtly powers the rhythm of the song, while his voice (something many never liked) pulls it in a different direction. The sum of the two is perfect bossa nova. This brief cut, with its lyrical flute coda and understated strings, stands as raw bossa; it would still have worked well stripped to simply guitar and voice. Unlike the diluted, slick version of the music that flooded the United States in the early 1960s, the emotion is evident in Gilberto's harsh voice, and the arrangement isn't afraid of a few rough edges; it's not trying to be pretty, but rather to say something. Jobim's gorgeous vocal melody works with Gilberto's limited range and, in fact, makes an advantage of it. In retrospect it's hard to understand the initial Brazilian outcry against Gilberto's singing, but it existed because he wasn't as melodic or obvious as the samba singers who predated him. Shocking at the time for the way it grated, his voice focused attention on the new style, in much the same way Elvis did for rock 'n' roll or Johnny Rotten for punk. Sweet but never syrupy in this combination, Gilberto and Jobim made a perfect pair.

"Get Up, Stand Up" (Bob Marley and the Wailers, 1975): The anthem of the downtrodden, written by Marley and former bandmate Peter Tosh, gets its best airing on *Live!* Looser than the studio version, it lets the excellent band vamp around the riff, while Marley, charismatic as the frontman, initiates an African-style call and response with the audience. It succeeds not only as one of the great reggae songs, memorable and meaningful, with the type of "conscious" lyric typical of the Rasta work of the era, but also as a live presentation; it's easy to feel yourself part of the audience, excited and at one with the performance. With the female I-Threes on backing vocals, Marley has a cushion behind his voice, and the musicians keep the rhythm going—which in this case is all the song needs. In many respects, it doesn't approach the quality of Marley's best work, but as a political statement (one that has been covered many, many times since), it's second to none.

"Toy Heart" (Bill Monroe and His Blue Grass Boys, 1946): Recorded after all the elements that made bluegrass had full coalesced, this particular track is unusual inasmuch as Monroe takes tenor, rather than lead, vocals. But his particular high, lonesome sound is immediately recognizable on this song. Kicking off with Monroe's supercharged, driving mandolin, guitarist Lester Flatt sings lead, while Earl Scruggs's trademark three-finger banjo workout is a powerful foil for Monroe's instrumental work. This was the first classic lineup of the Blue Grass Boys, and in it the music Monroe has visualized came to fruition in a uniquely American style. It borrowed from country and from the Appalachian music that had been born across the Atlantic, but in this guise it was something completely fresh. The harmonies had no Celtic or English equivalent, and the forceful pace of much of the music had a completely American energy. Monroe had also come into his own as a writer, churning out a series of excellent pieces that played to the strengths of his musicians, letting their skills flow—although Monroe made sure no one eclipsed his position at the front and center.

SIX

World Music on CD

W orld music is so vast that to try and capture it on fifty, or even one hundred, CDs is a difficult task. The albums listed in this chapter are simply entry points into world music, places from which further exploration can begin. A few almost choose themselves, but the majority take more consideration, and might not always be as obvious.

A simpler way might be to pick a number of compilations. Apart from offering more bang for the buck, they bring a wider selection of artists to the ears. And in some cases, compilations can be ideal. The problem is it takes more than one track to understand an artist. There are compilations in this list, but they're few and far between; where they do occur, they tend to be of the single-artist variety, and then only because most of their catalog is difficult to obtain in the United States.

Much the same applies to multidisc sets. They represent a commitment of both time and money that most people are reluctantly hesitant to make. In a few rare cases, though, a particular set is worthwhile for the way it presents an artist.

The last factor to be considered is availability. Only a fraction of all world music finds release in the United States, and some exemplary discs never find domestic distribution, making them both difficult and expensive to obtain. So the parameters set are that the record must be issued in the United States and currently in print.

At least in America and Europe, they don't suffer from the pirating that's endemic in so many other places. In most parts of the globe, it's not unusual for pirated copies of CDs or cassettes—and throughout Africa and Asia, the cassette remains the main way of listening to music—to be in shops and on market stalls before the real album is officially released. And, of course, the artist sees no money from them. They're often identical to the authentic item in every detail except price, and in economies where money is tight at best and recorded music is a luxury, price counts.

Countering that is difficult; it might even prove impossible. And it certainly makes it harder for an artist to live from music alone. It's a thought to consider when you're budgeting for your next purchase.

Africa and the Middle East

Apocalypse across the Sky, The Master Musicians of Jajouka (Axiom, 1992): A crystalline recording of the Master Musicians, rather than the psychedelic woozy imposed by Brian Jones. This primal trance music doesn't need any enhancement to set the mind going. Taped on their home turf in Morocco in 1991, producer Bill Laswell does a masterful job of capturing the deep, earthy moods of the ensemble. To hear this is to feel as if you were there in the Rif Mountains and part of something spiritual. Under the leadership of Bachir Attir, the Master Musicians have never sounded more vibrant; the music jumps out of the speakers and surrounds you.

Caravanserai, Istanbul Oriental Ensemble (Network, 2001): Intended as a journey through an oasis town, this Turkish gypsy music is absolutely mesmerizing. All of the players are virtuosos (if you think a five-minute darbuka drumming solo might be boring, you just haven't heard Burhan Öçal), and they unleash their skills on these pieces that evoke the many moods of the Middle East. From the delicate to the driving, this is an exercise is musical brilliance, with the kanun (or *qanun*, a type of hammer dulcimer) especially outstanding. It's a shining insight into one particular stand of the Romany diaspora.

Classics, Oum Kalsoum (album credited to Omme Kolsoum) (EMI, 2001): Given her status as the greatest Arab vocalist of the twentieth century, it's a crime that so little of Oum Kalsoum's (also spelled Um Kulthum, Oum Kalthoum) music has been released in the United States; the diva of Egypt is poorly represented. There's no good, career-spanning anthology, but it's hard enough to find *any* of her music. This isn't perfect (none of her work with the marvelous Mohamed Abdel Wahab, for instance), but her art is very much intact. Her control, enunciation, and decoration of a line or phrase (all highly prized qualities in Arab classical music) is exquisite throughout.

Éthiopiques, Volume 1, Various Artists (Buda, 1998): Francis Falceto's ongoing investigation of the golden years of modern Ethiopian music (currently at nineteen discs) started off with a bang, delving into the catalog of Ahma Records and coming up with some gems. The roots are deep and local, but this is definitely 1970s pop music, with a soulful groove that could easily have come from the Stax label in its heyday. But listen to the blues-like tezeta of Gétachew Kassa, melancholy and haunting, or Tèshomè Meteki's "Yèzèmèd Yèbaed," where you'll hear echoes of early Santana. Fascinating.

JuJu Music, King Sunny Adé and His African Beats (Mango, 1982): Adé's first international release was meant to make him a star; and to that end, both material and playing are red hot. The downside is that you don't get the extended tracks that have always been typical of his performance, but even the abbreviated dialogs between instruments and percussion are a joy, striking at the heart of juju music. Once the pedal steel kicks in, it often hits another level altogether, while Adé's dry, assertive lead guitar is wonderfully sharp.

Mali: Cordes Anciennes, Various Artists (Buda, 1970): This was the first album devoted solely to the West African harp called the kora. Featuring five outstanding players in different combinations, it illustrates perfectly the rippling flow of the instrument and the ways it's used in Mande music. Lyrically seductive, it's more aggressive than the Western harp but equally capable of nuance and softness. If a single instrument can define a culture, then the kora defines the Mande. Glowing performances and complete virtuosity combine to warrant a classic tag for this disc.

Miss Perfumado, Cesaria Evora (Nonesuch, 1992): This is the disc that propelled the Cape Verdean diva to star status in world music, and it's easy to understand why. Her lived-in voice, seductively glorious and whisky-soaked, caresses the songs. There's Brazil in the rhythms, Portuguese fado in the guitar, and the piano and strings add a serenity to the sound. She's the perfect interpreter of the island morna style, which evokes so many other things, but grabs at the heart in its aching. "Sodade" alone is worth the price of admission, but everything else glimmers, too.

The Best Best of Fela Kuti, Fela Kuti (MCA, 1999): The temptation is to choose a single album, if only because this two-disc set offers edited versions of some pieces. But this really does contain plenty of Kuti's greatest, dynamic Afrobeat songs. There are full versions of "Lady," "Zombie," and others, showing how politically uncompromising and confrontational he could be lyrically. The music, utterly irresistible, with Tony Allen's drumming a revelation, has grooves a mile wide, their riffs interlocking under jazz improvisations. It makes for an excellent point of entry into Kuti's massive catalog.

The Indestructible Beat of Soweto, Various Artists (Shanachie, 1986): One of the Ur-texts of world music, this release from South Africa first broadcast the soulful, danceable mbaqanga music of the townships around the world. Whether it's the growling bass voice of Mahlathini, the glorious Zulu harmonies of Ladysmith Black Mambazo, or epic workouts on guitar or accordion over wonderfully elastic bass playing, this still stands as incredibly alive, raw music with an undeniable power. Its historical importance is overshadowed only by the music within.

The Music in My Head, Various Artists (Stern's, 1998): Intended as a "soundtrack" to the book of the same name by Mark Hudson, this compilation of African music from the 1970s and early 1980s stands as testament to a truly golden age. There's a young Youssou N'Dour, singing as if his life depended on it, some wonderful stuff from Salif Keita, and also the great Franco. The standout, however, is "Boubou N'Gary," by Senegal's Étoile 2000, which sounds as if the Yardbirds had brought their psychedelic fuzz to West Africa, with dub master Lee Perry producing—completely mad and utterly brilliant.

The Rough Guide to Youssou N'Dour & Étoile de Dakar, Youssou N'Dour and Étoile de Dakar (World Music Network, 2002): This is N'Dour before he became an international superstar and world music's brightest flame. All the compositions are his, from the late 1970s and early 1980s. There's plenty to love in his later work, too, but this documents N'Dour and the band shaping and perfecting their mbalax. It's raw and energized, with a rich, youthful fire. N'Dour's griot wail simply unleashes throughout on tracks that captured his native Senegalese market.

The Rough Guide to Raï, Various Artists (World Music Network, 2002): Raï might not be Algeria's only music, but it's certainly the dominant one. The focus here is on the electric pop-raï of the 1980s, which rejuvenated the more traditional form and made it more instantly accessible. There's excellent early material from Cheb Khaled, long considered the King of Raï, Cheb Mami, and Cheba Zahouania, but it delves back further for Bellemou in the 1960s and the ragged voice of Cheikha Remitti, one of raï's seminal figures. As an introduction to the modern sound, this is probably unrivaled.

The Very Best of the Rumba Giant of Zaire, Franco (Manteca, 2000): Franco's albums are hard to come by in America, making this compilation especially desirable. This does a very good job, ranging from "On Entre OK, On Sort KO," in the early years of OK Jazz when the Congolese rumba was still taking concrete shape, to his last great recording, "Attention Na Sida," in 1987. In between comes some excellent songwriting but, more important, plenty of his exceptional guitar work—enough to understand why he was dubbed "The Sorcerer of the Guitar."

Asia

Anokha, Soundz of the Asian Underground, Various Artists (Quango, 1997): Talvin Singh's Anokha club in London was the first widely distributed expression of the Asian Underground movement, which mixed Indian music with electronica, breakbeats, and hip-hop in a seamless, majestic fusion. This sampler not only features Singh himself (a tabla master), but adventurous, groundbreaking work from State of Bengal, the great young Bollywood composer A. R. Rahman, and several others. Since then the underground has gone overground and become the Asian Massive.

Explorer Series—Indonesia, Various Artists (Nonesuch, 2003): These twelve discs, recorded in the field between the mid-1960s and early 1980s, are a miraculous source of music. There's gamelan from Bali and Java, including the glorious, stately court gamelan style, music for the classic Shadow Play, the vocal styles of the South Pacific Islands, and the strange popular music of west Java, among others. This is ethnomusicological work that steps outside academia; the music is eminently accessible, well-documented in a nonfussy manner, and thoroughly addictive.

Master of Sitar, Ravi Shankar (Nascente, 2001): India's sitar genius needs little introduction. But while many know his name, few have delved into his work. This compilation of vintage material is an excellent place to begin. With a raga for each time of day, there's a full range of moods, from the contemplative to the blistering, accompanied by superb tabla players, including his own teacher, Ustad Alla Rakha. Shankar's genius is as much in his formal presentation of the music as in his improvisation, and this showcases both facets perfectly.

Music of Indonesia, Volume 20: Indonesian Guitars, Various Artists (Smithsonian Folkways, 1999): A bit of an oddity, perhaps, but a delightful one. The guitar probably arrived with the Portuguese several centuries ago and was promptly absorbed into Indonesian folk culture, either as a standard six-string model or in different homemade configurations. This glimpse into many different styles is illuminating, not merely as a look at myriad Indonesian folk and pop styles, from a cover of a dangdut hit on a two-string electrified kacapi to a piece that sounds as if it could have stepped straight out of Appalachia.

Music for the Gods, Various Artists (Rykodisc, 1995): This is a record that works on two levels, as both a historical document (recorded in 1940–1941) and a magical exploration of Indonesian gamelan music. While much of it comes from Bali, whose gamelan tradition differs from other parts of the archipelago, there are other styles shown. Considering the difficult recording conditions, Bruce and Sheridan Fahnestock did a job that's little short of miraculous. Gamelan is well represented on the Nonesuch *Explorer Series Indonesia*, but these early tracks hold an unspoiled magic that's almost timeless in its magic.

Paris Concerts Complete, Volumes 1–5, Nusrat Fateh Ali Khan (Ocora, 2001): Some performers need space for their art to come fully alive; the late Nusrat Fateh Ali Khan was one of them. These discs, recorded in France in the 1980s when he was on the cusp of global stardom, are perhaps as close to perfection as he ever came in his Sufi qawwali art. The first two discs show him very much a part of his "party," with wonderful little vocal improvisations. The others, recorded three years later, show a man of full confidence with a deeper voice and more meditative style.

Peppermint Tea House, Shoukichi Kina (Luaka Bop, 1994): Kina, the founder of Champloose, is the godfather of modern Okinawan music. A powerful singer and composer, he combines the pumping drive of rock with local melodies and influences, including some fabulous shamisen. This compilation covers a healthy chunk of his career, including tracks from his 1980 collaboration with Ry Cooder. Ranging from the lighthearted to the challengingly dense, Kina is the seed from which contemporary Okinawan music has grown. It's all engagingly accessible, with many rewards.

Rapa Iti, The Tahitian Choir (Shanachie, 1992): South Pacific vocal music can be both unnerving and moving, and this manages to be both. The massed voices weave a complex web of sounds, working in microtonal scales that slip and swoop at unexpected movements, to the point at which you might think your CD player is malfunctioning. It's not; this is simply one of the dangerous joys of discovering this music. It takes some adjustment, but one of the pleasures of world music is the way it can expose you to the unexpected—which this does in spades.

The Rough Guide to Bollywood, Various Artists (World Music Network, 2002): Although there's a heavy bias to R. D. Burman in the music here, this proves to be a fairly well-weighted assessment of modern Bollywood. The kitsch element is toned down in favor of catchy melodies—although here and there the Cuisinarting of Western and Eastern styles remains apparent. There's no A. R. Rahman, which is a sad omission, but allow for that and you'll be happy. All the great playback singers are here, including the legendary Asha Bhosle and Lata Mangeshkar, and newer names like Lucky Ali.

The Silk Road, A Musical Caravan, Various Artists (Smithsonian Folkways, 2002): Under the auspices of classical cellist Yo-Yo Ma, the music of the Silk Road has been explored lately. This two-disc set, made up of modern field recordings, chronicles both the art music of master musicians and the folk music of ordinary people. By example, it shows how traditions have traveled and bled into one another from China to the Middle East. But it's far more than an academic exercise; this is glorious, vibrant stuff, with some inspired playing and singing that makes every track a joy.

Where Young Grass Grows, Huun-Huur-Tu (Shanachie, 1999): Huun-Huur-Tu is the brand name in Tuvan throat singing for a reason—they're among the very best. But they're equally adept at local folk songs and outstanding instrumentalists, making them a triple threat. All three talents are exhibited here, although it's the unearthly overtone singing, in all its styles, that's the big attraction. This disc is a standout for its expressiveness, and the skill and sensitivity of the group—a high point in a glittering career. The throat singing is outstanding, but so is everything else, revealing Huun-Huur-Tu to be completely multidimensional in their achievements.

Europe

Band of Gypsies, Taraf de Haïdouks (Nonesuch, 2001): A live recording by what might be the best Balkan Gypsy band. With almost superhuman instrumental powers, and a playful sense of entertainment, the Romanians bring out several guests, including the excellent Koçani Orkestar Gypsy Brass Band for nothing less than a celebration of Romany music. It's guaranteed to raise your heartbeat several notches as they negotiate the complex times and twisting melodies with absolute ease. The record is a stunning achievement that's absolutely intoxicating.

Best Of, Mano Negra (Ark 21, 1997): France's Mano Negra was where Manu Chao honed his subversive skills, mixing up languages and musical styles—from North African to rockabilly—over a thundering political punk backdrop heavily influenced by the Clash. As a solo artist he's become a major name, but little beats the throb and energy of his late band at their best on "King King Five," "Indios De Barcelona," or "King of Bongo." This is the point where rock and world music truly intersect in a powerful polyglot of languages.

Aitara, Värttinä (Xenophile, 1994): With this disc Finland's Värttinä begins to step outside purely traditional music, although their own compositions are heavily influenced by the tradition. The keening vocals and harmonies are a trademark sound, intense and demanding, but for the first time their band takes equal prominence, coming into their own as an instrumental unit, so that everything is firing on all cylinders. Unusual at times (like sax and accordion together), but with an abundant sense of history, this stands as one of the highest points in Värttinä's ongoing evolution.

Black Rock, Djivan Gasparyan and Michael Brook (Real World, 1998): Armenia's duduk master teams up with a Canadian producer for a disc that highlights the soulfulness and sensuality of his oboe-like instrument. Brook's largely ambient arrangements leave the focus on Gasparyan, giving him a great deal of freedom, which he uses wisely (and his singing is also excellent). A fascinating hybrid of ancient and modern sounds that works, in large part, because of Gasparyan's connectedness to his

Armenian heritage. Eclectic in outlook, and beautifully played, this is true art-folk music.

Bohême de Cristal, Lo'Jo (World Village, 2001): The sound of modern, multicultural France on a single disc. Lo'Jo bring together edgy chanson with flailing Gypsy violin and the sounds of North and West Africa, and put it all into a heady brew, gleefully stirred by singer and leader Denis Péan. It's a record that breaks all the rules, but is absolutely intense and convincing throughout, the result of well over fifteen years of work by the band. Lo'Jo is like no one else; the detailed (yet free) arrangements are stunning, as is the writing.

Coolfin, Donal Lunny (Metro Blue, 1998): Lunny has become a ubiquitous figure in Irish music, and for this album he brought in some of the top instrumental and vocal talent around—a supergroup of sorts, and not all from the Emerald Isle (nor, indeed, is all the music). His own demanding compositions sit easily next to the traditional material, although he lets his famed bouzouki playing take a back seat. There's simply nothing to fault on this disc—superbly arranged, brilliantly played, a state-of-the-art manifesto of modern Celtic music.

Felenfeber: Norwegian Fiddle Fantasia, Annbjørg Lien (Shanachie, 1994): Lien's international debut after her appearance on *The Sweet Sunny North* is a glowing exercise on how to play the Norwegian national instrument, the hardangefele. It's more about tone rather than speed (although she's capable of that, as the tricky "The Plucked Halling" ably illustrates). A mix of traditional and modern tunes finds her in sparkling form, with the exuberance of youth and a mature technique—a powerful combination. It remains one of the best albums of Norwegian fiddle music around.

Le Mystère des Voix Bulgares, Le Mystère des Voix Bulgares (Nonesuch, 1989): A powerfully popular album at the beginning of the 1990s, this wasn't the work of a single group, but a collective name given to several choirs, their work pulled from the archives of Bulgarian Radio and Television by Swiss Marcel Cellier. Sources be damned: it's the glorious diaphonic harmonies that entrance, singing like no other, and it's indeed mysterious—they use a particular local singing technique. The material truly does come from the Bulgarian villages and keeps alive a deep tradition that communicates across language and culture.

Lost Souls, Spaccanapoli (Real World, 2000): Named for a street that used to divide Naples, Spaccanapoli use the rhythm of the tarantella and the tammariata, while still making strong socialist points in their lyrics (they grew out of a workers' collective). The basic group is heavily augmented on this debut, but their sound is never overwhelmed, as the Neopolitan harmonies emerge through the folk textures. The eerie title track is a standout, a journey into local mythology and culture, and singer Monica Pinto is a gauzy revelation throughout.

No Roses, Shirley Collins and the Albion Country Band (Mooncrest, 1971): Here's where England's folk traditionalists and the younger electric folkies came together. Behind Shirley Collins's artlessly affecting voice, some of the top folk talent created arrangements that pushed at the boundaries of what had been done in electric folk (listen to "Murder of Maria Marten," for example), without ever losing sense of why they were doing it. The balance of old and new is exact, the songs treated with respect but updated in the true folk manner. The apex of 1970s British folk-rock.

Post-Scriptum, Cristina Branco (L'Empreinte Digitate, 2001): Possibly the finest young Portuguese fadista, with a crystalline voice and an understated yet emotional singing style. She's not strictly traditional, but her music doesn't suffer in the least for that. With the excellent Custódio Castelo taking care of Portuguese guitar and arrangements, she can shine as a vocalist, singing lyrics written by modern poets. To hear her is an exquisite experience; the opening track "Ai Vida" is all it takes to convince the listener that Branco is a remarkable talent.

The Rough Guide to the Music of Greece, Various Artists (World Music Network, 2001): With the emphasis on three styles—the working-class grit of rembetika, the lush folk emtechno, and the poppier laïkó—this is an excellent survey, ranging from the traditional to the contemporary. The vintage Kostas Nouras track is excellent, and even Mikis Theodorakis (*Zorba the Greek*) is justifiably here as a folk musician. Most of Greece's major musical figures are represented, and the performances often carry all the headiness of a glass of retsina.

The Well below the Valley, Planxty (Shanachie, 1973): All the elements that made up Planxty—bouzouki, pipes, whistles, voices— were in perfect harmony for this release. They changed the face of Irish traditional music, and it's easy to hear why. They brought the energy and passion of rock to traditional music, while still allowing its delicacy to shine (as on "Hewlett"). Both Christy Moore and Andy Irvine were in fine form as singers, and Donal Lunny's bouzouki (at that point still a recent addition to Irish music) is quicksilver in its brilliance.

Trä, Hedningarna (Northside, 1994): As dark as a long midnight, with some disturbing samples amid some fabulous playing and singing, this disc nibbles hard at the edges of Swedish folk music. It takes plenty of sonic chances, but never loses the traditional root of the music. One of the heralds of the new Swedish folk sound, it's daring, but everything is here for a reason—to push the song home. The electronic overlay never obscures the fact that these are also world-class musicians and vocalists with a deep knowledge of the tradition—and brilliant imaginations.

Americas

Brazil Classic 1: Beleza Tropical, Various Artists (Luaka Bop, 1989): A strong compilation of post-*tropicália* MPB, or Brazilian popular music. Veloso, Gil, Nascimento, Buarque, and others represent the apex of writing skills, and the eighteen cuts cover a good range. As an introduction to (relatively) modern MPB, it never puts a foot wrong, even when it introduces some left-field artists, like Lô Borges. Kudos to David Byrne for putting this anthology together; it's the ideal way to dip your toes into the warm Brazilian waters.

Buena Vista Social Club, Various Artists (World Circuit/Nonesuch, 1997): Simply one of the great albums of modern world music, although its spirit harks back more than half a century. All the classic Cuban styles are here, performed by people who've been doing it for years. Lush, but never overarranged, brilliantly played and sung, it's a disc that deserves all the plaudits and sales, justifiably making global stars of several of its artists. It serves as the perfect primer of Cuban music, or you can just listen and be entranced.

Cajun Volume 1: Abbeville Breakdown 1929–1939, Various Artists (Columbia, 1991): This collection of archival Cajun recordings goes right to the heart of the music. Raw, often primal, it's remarkable stuff. Essentially made up of tracks by the Beaux Freres (along with their sister, Cleoma, and her husband, Joe Falcon), and also the Alley Boys of Abbeville, the twenty-two cuts here—several of which have never been released before— are an insight into history, a snapshot of Cajun music in the 1930s before it developed into today's more sophisticated form.

Corridos Prohibidos, Los Tigres del Norte (Fonovisa, 1989): Los Tigres had made the first real narcocorrido (Mexican drug smuggling ballad) in 1972, starting a whole genre. Here they return to it and up the stakes on all those who've copied their style. The norteño music, rhythmic and accordion driven, is perfect for the songs, letting the words flow. And what words—"El Zorro de Ojinaga" is perfect folk music. But there's also a social conscience at work here, although it's never didactic.

Dance Mania, Tito Puente (RCA, 1958): Tito Puente at the very height of his powers and popularity. Mambos, cha-cha-chas, boleros, and all the prevalent Latin styles get an energetic workout, with plenty of outstanding instrumental and vocal work. This is exactly what it claims to be—dance music (and in stereo)—and more than forty years on it stands against anything that's been released since. Puente has rarely sounded so good; the music leaps out of the speakers.

Etsi Shon (Grandfather Song), Jerry Alfred and the Medicine Beat (Red House, 1996): From Canada's Selkirk tribe, Alfred makes contemporary music with a thick traditional heartbeat. Singing mostly in his native Tutchone, Alfred and his band create gorgeous soundscapes around the drumbeat. Even the more conventional material, such as the title track, possesses an unusual power. The lyrics have an almost mythological depth, but throughout it's the drum that's at the center of things, recorded so closely you can hear creak and buzz of the skin.

High Lonesome, The Story of Bluegrass Music, Various Artists (CMH, 1994): The soundtrack to a film about bluegrass, this is one of the best compilations of a truly American music, with cuts by Bill Monroe, Ralph Stanley, Jimmy Martin, the Osborne Brothers, and others. More authentic and hardcore than *O Brother Where Art Thou?*, this goes for the jugular, celebrating that keening singing, rural sensibility, and the driving playing that exemplify bluegrass. Stunning performances throughout, even though most of them are more recent.

Klassic Kitchener Volume 3, Lord Kitchener (Ice, 1994): One of the greatest of all Trinidad's calypsonians, Lord Kitchener (Aldwyn Roberts) was the toast of the Road March for many years, and also enjoyed a successful career in England in the 1950s. This compilation includes two of his biggest tracks— "Tribute to Simon Spree" and "Sugar Bum Bum," his venture into soca—in addition to some of his compositions for steel pan, for which he was equally renowned. Every cut is superb, a glimpse into the art of calypso from a master.

Live in Bahia, Caetano Veloso (Nonesuch, 2002): Veloso's become a musical and intellectual icon in his native Brazil, an artist whose audience crosses generations. This two-CD live set, recorded in his native Bahia, is a perfect illustration of why he's so revered. It's a mix of new and classic Veloso songs, with wonderfully sympathetic arrangements and performances that bring out their essence. Not only a masterful writer, Veloso's matured into a softly majestic singer with an understated charisma. Short of a good best-of collection, this is the ideal way to experience his depth and breadth.

Susana Baca, Susana Baca (Luaka Bop, 1997): For many years Baca has investigated the history of Afro-Peruvian music as both a scholar and artist. Her international debut is the result of her study and inspiration, and it's nothing less than sensational. Accompanied solely by guitar and the rhythm box called the cajon (with panpipes on one track), her voice is sweetly sensual, a beautiful instrument she uses in a gloriously understated fashion. Much of the material is traditional and well served by Baca's interpretations, but even her performances of more modern pieces shimmer.

Tango: Zero Hour, Astor Piazzolla (Pangaea, 1992): The culmination of Piazzolla's work in tango, this disc pulls together all the elements of his music to become a persuasive manifesto for his nuevo tango ideas. The playing, by Piazzolla himself on bandoneon backed by his quintet, is impeccable. His compositions, often dark and moody, are perfect nighttime creations.

Tougher than Tough: The Story of Jamaican Music, Various Artists (Island, 1993): A comprehensive and absolutely indispensable history of Jamaican music from 1958 to 1993, taking in local R&B, ska, rock steady, reggae, toasting, dub, dancehall, and ragga. Virtually every important track in Jamaican music is here, whether it's "Easy Snappin'" or "Under My Sleng Teng." Bob Marley is represented twice, once with "No Woman No Cry," the unofficial Jamaican anthem. With excellent notes by Steve Barrow, this tells you everything you need about Jamaican music.

SEVEN

The Language of
World Music

There is, of course, no single language of world music. That makes any comprehensive glossary virtually impossible, and the following makes no claim other than to cover some of the main terms you'll encounter, whether it's a type of music, a rhythm, or an instrument. It's not unusual for an instrument, for example, to be essentially the same in different areas, but with different names—just to compound the linguistic problem. In those cases, the dominant name (i.e., the one by which it's generally known) is used.

A Cappella: Sung without instrumental accompaniment.

Benga: East African musical style (most popular in Kenya), where guitar lines imitate the *nyatiti* lyre over heavily syncopated rhythms.

Bhangra: Originally a Punjabi harvest dance, revolving around the sound of the dhol drum. In Britain it became more of a pop form, with Western instruments, and very popular with Asian youth.

Bossa Nova: Literally "New Beat"; the invention of Brazilian Antonio Carlos Jobim in the 1950s, wedding the rhythm of samba to jazz.

Calypso: West Indian song form with African origins, associated primarily with Trinidad and Tobago. Typified by humorous or topical lyrics, it can be accompanied by guitar, orchestra, or steel pan band.

Cheikh (f.: cheikha): An honorific term used in raï to mark an elder or veteran. Younger male singers are called chebs, and females, chebas.

Cimbalon: A kind of hammer dulcimer, popular throughout the Balkans. The Middle Eastern variant is the qanum.

Congolese Rumba: Variant on the Cuban rumba rhythm, especially popular in Congo, but which also found favor throughout the continent.

Cumbia: Colombia's most popular traditional dance rhythm, now used throughout Latin music. Essentially a simple, one-bar rhythm with a strong backbeat, it combines African rhythms with Hispanic melodies and Native Indian harmonies.

Dangdut: The pervasive Indonesian pop form characterized by a low beat closing one bar and a high beat starting the next.

Djeli (f.: dejlimuso): The Malian and Guinean term for griot.

Fado: Literally "fate," this is the yearning music of Portugal, specifically working-class Lisbon. With poetic lyrics and generally a stripped-down musical backing, it deals with the acceptance of life's ill luck.

Flamenco: Spanish music of Gypsy origin that developed in Andalusia. Originally a vocal and dance music, the guitar arrived later.

Gamelan: Refers to the grouping of percussion instruments and metallophones. Found in Indonesia, there are two main types of gamelan: the slower, meditative Javanese and the more energetic Balinese.

Griot (f.: griotte): In West Africa, griots are the traditional singing caste that keeps the oral histories of families and communities.

Highlife: Dance music that originated in the early twentieth century in Ghana. It developed into separate urban and rural styles, the rural being more acoustic and folk, the urban more electric. Also popular in Nigeria.

Jeel (also je'el): From the Arabic, literally "youth music," it's an offshoot of sha'bi, a more pop-oriented style aimed at Arab teens.

Joik: The impressionistic singing of the Sami (or Lapp) people, usually songs about things, places, or people, rather than emotions.

Juju: A Nigerian Yoruba musical form that developed during the first few decades of the twentieth century, characterized by dialogs between melodic and rhythmic instruments over a tight groove.

Kantele: A type of zither found throughout the Baltic; the number of strings can vary.

Klezmer: Originally the music of Eastern European Ashkenazic Jews, it mingled freely with Balkan and Romany music. Played by Jewish immigrants in early-twentieth-century America, it proved briefly popular, and has undergone a revival since the late 1980s.

Kora: Harp-like instrument, usually with twenty-one strings; found mostly in Senegal, Gambia, Mali, and Guinea.

Kwaito: Modern South African style that draws from hip-hop, house music, and disco, merging them with more rooted forms.

Maqām (or makam): The modes or scales used in Arabic music. There are nine main groups with forty-two major maqāms, although many more exist.

Marrabenta: The urban dance music style of Mozambique. It originated in the south of the country but was repressed by the Portuguese until independence in 1975.

Mbalax: The Senegalese rhythm builds on cross-ryhthms traditionally used in talking-drum ensembles, taking dialogs between drums and voices and giving the parts to guitars and keyboard. They play over the rhythm, while the talking drum (sabar) interjects comments.

Mbaqanga: Black South African township music, first heard in the 1930s, but coming to prominence in the late 1950s, characterized by a powerful bass underpinning. Grew out of pennywhistle jive to become the predominant pop form. The jit style of Zimbabwe is very similar.

Mbira: Thumb piano, made of tuned metal keys in a gourd or wooden box. The same instrument has different names in different parts of Africa—mbira is the term used in Zimbabwe.

Merengue: Latin rhythm that originated in the Dominican Republic and which has now become pan-Latin.

Morna: The Cape Verdean song form popularized by Cesaria Evora. Full of melancholy and wistfulness, it's influenced by fado, West African, and Brazilian music, giving a softly syncopated rhythm to the minor key, yearning melodies.

Narcocorrido: Modern Mexican folk ballad (or corrido), performed by *norteño* bands, with subject matter revolving around narcotics trafficking and violence.

Norteño (or tejano or Tex-Mex): Accordion-based music from the Mexico-Texas border area, influenced by the polka music of German settlers in the region.

Nyckelharpa: A Swedish instrument, bowed like a fiddle, but notes are achieved by depressing keys.

Oud: Lute-like instrument popular throughout the Middle East, usually with five or six double courses of strings. Variations occur from China to Western Europe.

Pipa: Ancient Chinese lute-like instrument (mentioned as far back as 200 B.C.E.) with four strings, a pear-shaped body, and thirty frets.

Polska: Swedish dance with a characteristic three-beat emphasis.

Qawwali: A term referring to both the musicians and the style of music. Sufi religious poetry set to music, aiming at ecstasy through singing.

Qin: Chinese zither with seven strings.

Raga (or raag)**:** The main Hindustani classical music, although ragas also occur in South Indian Carnatic music. A large number of ragas exist for different times of day, with different moods. Each has a prescribed tonal line and framework, while leaving room for improvisation.

Raï: Algerian music that began as the sound of the underclass in the city of Oran. Developed from acoustic to electric music, and gained international popularity, but remains socially unacceptable in Algeria.

Ranchera: Nostalgic urban Mexican music that harks back to simpler, rural ways.

Reggae: Jamaican musical style that developed in the late 1960s from ska and rock steady. Easily identifiable by the accents of the second and fourth beats of the bar.

Rembetika: Greek urban, working-class music. The songs are often about death, oppression, and crime—the lot of the lower classes, accepted with resignation.

Runo-song: An ancient Finnish musical song form, with eight syllables per line and rhyming syllables in the beginning of each word on a line. The songs themselves are generally short.

Salegy: Relative modern rhythm from Madagascar, performed both electrically and acoustically. Almost always fast-paced, the 6/8 rhythm makes it stand out.

Salsa: Pan-Latin rhythm that's made up of any number of other Latin rhythms, and probably the predominant Latin style outside Latin pop.

Samba: *The* versatile Brazilian rhythm, which comes in many forms. Developed from the choro but with a heavy layer of Afro-Brazilian syncopation. Heavily identified with the annual Río de Janeiro carnaval, where samba schools from different districts compete.

Saudade: Translates from Portuguese as "sadness," a quality endemic to both Cape Verdean morna and Portuguese fado.

Sha'bi (also chaa bi): The raw street pop style popular across North Africa and the Middle East. Originating in Cairo in the 1920s, it's become more of generic pop form in recent years, with many of the rough edges smoothed down and the lyrics cleaned up for mass consumption.

Shamisen: Japanese three-string lute. It originated in Okinawa but was brought to the mainland four hundred years ago. Features heavily in both the classical and folk traditions.

Sitar: Indian plucked instrument with a gourd resonator. It has four melodic strings, with three more drone strings, plus nine to thirteen sympathetic strings. The frets on the neck are movable.

Sizhu: The predominant folk music style of south China, also known as silk and bamboo, because of the bamboo flutes and plucked and bowed instruments using silk strings.

Slack Key Guitar: Hawaiian finger-picked guitar style, so named because of the many different tuning possibilities, which involve slackening off the keys to change the tone.

Son: Son is the main musical force in Cuba, the root of much of the music. These days it takes many musical forms.

Soukous: Essentially a speeded-up form of Congolese rumba, popular on European dance floors in the late 1970s and early 1980s.

Tabla: A set of two small hand drums used in Indian music. The heads are made of skin, but covered with a paste made from flour and iron filings.

Tango: A dance commonly associated with Argentina, whose origins lie in the West Indies and Africa.

Taqsim (or taksim): In Arabic music, an introductory improvisation that sets the mood for the piece, working within the maqam that will be used.

Throat Singing: A term for overtone singing of several different types, where harmonics either above or below the sung note are also produced in the throat. Found mostly in Central Asia but also in the chanting of Tibetan monks.

Tres: Cuban guitar-like instrument with three sets of strings.

Tropicália: Movement in Brazil in the mid-1960s, aimed at shaking up attitudes by introducing elements of rock and other styles, with electric instruments, making the music less nationalistic.

Zouk: Music of the French Antilles, with roots in the Caribbean, Europe, and Africa. Meaning "party" in Creole, it's typified by a loping dance beat.

Resources for Curious Listeners

World music is a still-emerging genre, which means that there aren't yet as many resources as there exist for other styles of music. However, the past few years have seen a rise in the number of books, magazines, and Web sites with information on world music artists, and the list keeps growing every day. Below are some of the best current resources for anyone interested in world music.

Books

Compared to other musical genres, world music is very poorly served by books. The majority of those that exist are academic, ethnomusicological texts—fascinating in their way but definitely not for the general reader. The books listed here escape the ghetto of academe, including a few single artist biographies of major figures.

Africa O-Ye, Graeme Ewens: This is an enthusiastic, well-written (and profusely illustrated) survey of African music that quickly gets to the essence of the continent.

Awakening Spaces, Brenda F. Berrian: An academic look at the music of the French Antilles, Berrian's book is dry in parts but is an important in-depth study nonetheless, covering all the important bases.

Bass Culture, Lloyd Bradley: An excellent history of reggae, this is as much a page-turner as any thriller.

Breakout: Profiles in African Rhythm, Gary Stewart: A little dated now (it was published in 1992), but it's still an excellent primer on major African music styles and artists.

Congo Colossus: The Life and Legacy of Franco and OK Jazz, Graeme Ewens: This superb biography of the Congolese "Sorcerer of the Guitar" is by one of the most knowledgeable writers on African music.

Fela, the Life and Times of an African Musical Icon, Michael E. Veal: The title sums it up—a biography of Nigeria's most turbulent musical figure, the influential inventor of Afrobeat who was silenced only by death.

In Griot Time, Banning Eyre: American journalist Eyre spent seven months in Bamako studying with the legendary guitarist from the Super Rail Band, Djelimady Tounkara. This book about his experiences goes beyond biography, diary, or travelog to capture much of the musical essence of Mali.

Mali Blues, Lieve Morris: Essentially a wonderful travel book, the long title piece is a biography of Mali's famed singer/songwriter, Boubacar Traoré.

MusicHound World, ed. Adam McGovern: A little dated now, and with some strange omissions (and inclusions), but it's a good biographical dictionary with sterling CD recommendations for each artist.

Narcocorrido, Elijah Wald: The first look at the popular Mexican narcocorrido form actually goes beyond that to become a study of modern corridos and the musicians who perform them, including some excellent interviews with the composers.

Popular Musics of the Non-Western World, Peter Manuel: The author, a professor of music, sets himself a massive task with the title but does a good job of briefly presenting a huge range of musical styles.

Rumba on the River, Gary Stewart: This is an extremely complete history of Congolese rumba and soukous by a man who appears to have heard every disc to have ever come out of the area. It is detailed and painstaking, but eminently readable.

Sweet Mother, Modern African Music, Wolfgang Bender: This excellent overview of African music from North to South is concise, smart, and fun and makes for an excellent introduction.

Tejano and Regional Mexican Music, Ramiro Burr: This biographical dictionary of the performers also covers the totality of Mexican regional music, the styles, and the chronology—a one-stop guide to the genre.

The Brazilian Sound, Chris McGown and Ricardo Pessanha: This is perhaps the single best book on Brazilian music, going through the histories, the styles, and the performers in a comprehensive fashion.

The Rough Guide to Reggae, Steve Barrow and Peter Dalton: This superbly detailed book on all facets of reggae, by two people who know the music inside and out, is the benchmark for all reggae books.

The Rough Guide to World Music, Volumes 1 and 2, ed. Simon Broughton, Mark Ellingham, and Richard Trillo: This is the Bible of world music, with almost everything you could want to know, excellent CD selections, and a great sense of both history and the present. It's knowledgeable without being dry. The pieces for each country are written by people who truly know the music—and who can communicate well.

The Voice of Egypt, Virginia Danielson: This long overdue biography of Um Kulthum, the greatest Arab diva of the twentieth century, is not perfect, but it transmits her greatness throughout.

Tropical Truth, a Story of Music and Revolution in Brazil, Caetano Veloso: Part autobiography, part history of the influential tropicália movement, and part musings on the Brazilian arts, Veloso's book offers an important (though sometimes dense) look at an important point in Brazil's modern musical history.

Magazines

Together the magazines listed below do an excellent job of keeping readers informed about the current scene in world and roots music, including both the latest trends and emerging stars, and classic sounds of the past.

Dirty Linen: Although it primarily covers folk music, this magazine includes plenty of world music CD reviews and occasional features on world music figures.

fRoots: Pronounced *eff-roots*, this British magazine has been around for more than two decades, before world music gained any widespread popularity. Hard to find in the United States, but worth tracking down, or subscribing to. It's published ten times a year, with a free compilation CD in each double issue.

Global Rhythm: The only U.S. magazine that solely covers world music and culture has come a long way in the past few years. These days it's a force on the world music magazine scene, with some good coverage of artists and events.

Penguin Eggs: This Canadian magazine that features folk music also peeks around the corner into world music from time to time.

Sing Out!: The granddaddy of U.S. magazines, with more than half a century under its belt, *Sing Out!*'s focus is folk music. But there's still plenty of world music coverage in the review section, and features on world performers are becoming more regular.

Songlines: This British magazine, put out by the people behind the *Rough Guide* music books, is published every other month and includes a free CD. It has good U.S. distribution and excellent content.

Radio

One of the best ways to be exposed to music from around the globe is online. Internet radio makes it possible to receive broadcasts from all over the world on your desktop. Some shows and stations can be excellent—this is a brief list, the mere tip of the iceberg. The more adventurous you are, the more you'll discover.

NPR (www.npr.org): National Public Radio covers world music very well, with interviews and reviews on shows like *Morning Edition*, *All Things Considered*, and *Fresh Air*. Also worth catching is news show *The World*.

BBC Radio 3 (www.bbc.co.uk/radio3/): Radio 3 carries several world music shows, including *Late Junction*, *World Routes*, and the estimable Andy Kershaw. Also well worth catching are the *Asian Network* and *World on Your Street*.

Charlie Gillett (http://www.bbc.co.uk/london/insideldn/radio/charlie_gillett.shtml): One of the best world music disk jockeys, Gillett is knowledgeable and passionate. His weekly show (which is archived at the site) offers mix of recorded music and live guests.

CBC Global Village (http://www.cbc.ca/globalvillage/): A weekly show on Canadian radio, *Global Village* offers a selection of features and music that's frequently fascinating and always enjoyable.

Web Sites

Many of the magazines in this chapter maintain Web sites, as do most record labels. And these days, many artists have their own Web sites. The following sites go beyond that to offer a broader range of information.

Afropop Worldwide (www.afropop.org): This superb site covers all aspects of African music, with radio, features, and reviews. It's comprehensive and informative.

Allmusic (www.allmusic.com): This site features biographies and reviews that are generally—but not always—accurate.

Global Sound (www.globalsound.org): Part of the Smithsonian, Global Sound is slowly putting music archives from around the world online, supplementing the music with plenty of background information. It's an important historical site.

Global Village Idiot (www.globalvillageidiot.net): This is a shameless plug for the author's world and roots music Webzine.

Mondomix (www.mondomix.org): The English-language version of this French site is always brimming with features, reviews, audio, and video—a broadband multimedia dream. This is one of the best European sites.

Rock Paper Scissors (www.rockpaperscissors.biz): A site run by a publicist, this is rapidly becoming a good, interesting resource for different types of world music.

Rootsworld (www.rootsworld.com): This is a subscription site, but with plenty of free content, including features and reviews, often augmented by audio. The site has excellent content, and frequent updates.

The Brazilian Sound (www.thebraziliansound.com): From the people who brought you the book on Brazil, this Web site covers everything Brazilian.

World Music Central (www.worldmusiccentral.org): This good, in-depth site covers the gamut of world music, with plenty of current news.

Index

About the Author

Chris Nickson was born and raised in Leeds, England, and now lives in the United States. He is a music journalist who writes frequently about world and roots music; his work has appeared in *CMJ, fRoots, Sing Out!, Wired, Saudi Aramco World,* and *Dirty Linen* and on Amazon.com, Allmusic.com, and Sonicnet.com. He also broadcasts regularly on NPR and CBC radio. Chris's "Legends of World Music" column appears monthly in *Global Rhythm* magazine. He runs the Web site globalvillageidiot.net, a source for information on world music.